T
174
· 3
· TRA

UNITED NATIONS CONFERENCE ON TRADE AND DEVELOPMENT

TRANSFER OF TECHNOLOGY

UNCTAD Series
on issues in international investment agreements

UNITED NATIONS
New York and Geneva, 2001

NOTE

UNCTAD serves as the focal point within the United Nations Secretariat for all matters related to foreign direct investment and transnational corporations. In the past, the Programme on Transnational Corporations was carried out by the United Nations Centre on Transnational Corporations (1975-1992) and the Transnational Corporations and Management Division of the United Nations Department of Economic and Social Development (1992-1993). In 1993, the Programme was transferred to the United Nations Conference on Trade and Development. UNCTAD seeks to further the understanding of the nature of transnational corporations and their contribution to development and to create an enabling environment for international investment and enterprise development. UNCTAD's work is carried out through intergovernmental deliberations, research and analysis, technical assistance activities, seminars, workshops and conferences.

The term "country" as used in this study also refers, as appropriate, to territories or areas; the designations employed and the presentation of the material do not imply the expression of any opinion whatsoever on the part of the Secretariat of the United Nations concerning the legal status of any country, territory, city or area or of its authorities, or concerning the delimitation of its frontiers or boundaries. In addition, the designations of country groups are intended solely for statistical or analytical convenience and do not necessarily express a judgement about the stage of development reached by a particular country or area in the development process.

The following symbols have been used in the tables:

Two dots (..) indicate that data are not available or are not separately reported. Rows in tables have been omitted in those cases where no data are available for any of the elements in the row;

A dash (-) indicates that the item is equal to zero or its value is negligible;

A blank in a table indicates that the item is not applicable;

A slash (/) between dates representing years, e.g. 1994-95, indicates a financial year;

Use of a hyphen (-) between dates representing years, e.g. 1994-1995, signifies the full period involved, including the beginning and end years.

Reference to "dollars" ($) means United States dollars, unless otherwise indicated.

Annual rates of growth or change, unless otherwise stated, refer to annual compound rates.

Details and percentages in tables do not necessarily add to totals because of rounding.

The material contained in this study may be freely quoted with appropriate acknowledgement.

UNCTAD/ITE/IIT/28

UNITED NATIONS PUBLICATION
Sales No. E.01.II.D.33
ISBN 92-1-112545-6

IIA Issues Paper Series

The main purpose of the UNCTAD Series on issues in international investment agreements – and other relevant instruments – is to address concepts and issues relevant to international investment agreements and to present them in a manner that is easily accessible to end-users. The series covers the following topics:

Admission and establishment
Competition
Dispute settlement (investor-State)
Dispute settlement (State-State)
Employment
Environment
Fair and equitable treatment
Foreign direct investment and development
Home country measures
Host country operational measures
Illicit payments
Incentives
International investment agreements: flexibility for development
Investment-related trade measures
Lessons from the MAI
Most-favoured-nation treatment
National treatment
Scope and definition
Social responsibility
State contracts
Taking of property
Taxation
Transfer of funds
Transfer of technology
Transfer pricing
Transparency
Trends in international investment agreements: an overview

Preface

The secretariat of the United Nations Conference on Trade and Development (UNCTAD) is implementing a work programme on international investment agreements. It seeks to help developing countries to participate as effectively as possible in international investment rule-making at the bilateral, regional, plurilateral and multilateral levels. The programme embraces capacity?building seminars, regional symposia, training courses, dialogues between negotiators and groups of civil society and the preparation of a Series of issues papers.

This paper is part of that Series. It is addressed to Government officials, corporate executives, representatives of non?governmental organizations, officials of international agencies and researchers. The Series seeks to provide balanced analyses of issues that may arise in discussions about international investment agreements. Each study may be read by itself, independently of the others. Since, however, the issues treated closely interact with one another, the studies pay particular attention to such interactions.

The Series is produced by a team led by Karl P. Sauvant and Pedro Roffe. The principal officer responsible for its production is Anna Joubin?Bret, who oversees the development of the papers at various stages. The members of the team include Christoph Spennemann and Jörg Weber. The Series' principal advisers are Arghyrios A. Fatouros, Sanjaya Lall, Peter T. Muchlinski and Patrick Robinson. The present paper is based on a manuscript prepared by Peter Muchlinski. Reprinted in the Appendix is the "Outcome" of an UNCTAD Expert Meeting on International Arrangements for Transfer of Technology held in Geneva from 27 to 29 June 2001. The annex table on technology transfer provisions in multilateral environment agreements was provided by Charles Arden-Clarke. The final version reflects comments received from Ümit D. Efendioglu, Assad Omer and Pedro Roffe. The paper was desktop-published by Teresita Sabico.

R. Ricupero

Geneva, October 2001   Secretary-General of UNCTAD

Acknowledgments

UNCTAD's work programme on international investment agreements is implemented by a team of UNCTAD staff members and consultants headed by Karl P. Sauvant, Khalil Hamdani and Pedro Roffe and including Marianela Bruno Pollero, Sylvia Constain, Arghyrios A. Fatouros, Anna Joubin-Bret, Sanjaya Lall, Peter T. Muchlinski, Patrick Robinson, Christopher Spennemann and Jörg Weber. Administrative support is provided by Séverine Excoffier.

UNCTAD has carried out a number of activities related to the work programme in co?operation with other intergovernmental organizations, including the Secretariat of the Andean Community, l'Agence pour la Francophonie, the Inter-Arab Investment Guarantee Corporation, the League of Arab States, the Organization of American States, la Secretaría de Integración Económica Centroamericana and the World Trade Organization. UNCTAD has also cooperated with non?governmental organizations, including the German Foundation for International Development, the Centro de Estudios Interdisciplinarios de Derecho Industrial y Económico Universidad de Buenos Aires, the Consumer Unity and Trust Society - India, the Economic Research Forum - Cairo, the European Roundtable of Industrialists, the Friedrich Ebert Foundation, the International Confederation of Free Trade Unions, Oxfam, SOMO - Centre for Research on Multinational Corporations, the Third World Network, la Universidad del Pacífico, the University of the West Indies, and World Wildlife Fund International.

Funds for the work programme have so far been received from Australia, Brazil, Canada, France, Japan, the Netherlands, Norway, Sweden, Switzerland, the United Kingdom and the European Commission. China, Egypt, Guatemala, India, Jamaica, Malaysia, Morocco, Peru, Sri Lanka and Venezuela have also contributed to the work programme by hosting regional symposia. All of these contributions are gratefully acknowledged.

Table of contents

Executive summary

This paper discusses the issue of technology transfer in the context of international investment agreements (IIAs). It is an issue that has generated debate for many years. Given the centrality of technology to development, and the necessity of technology acquisition by developing countries as a means of furthering development, it is desirable that such countries should be able to benefit from the generation, transfer and diffusion of the best available technology. Unfortunately, this has not always been the case. In particular, the fact that most of the world's advanced technology is generated privately by transnational corporations (TNCs), whose principal research and development (R&D) activity is located in developed countries, creates an asymmetry between technology possession and the location of technological need. The result is a gap between the technology developed and owned by firms in developed countries and that which can be obtained and utilized by developing countries.

This reality has generated numerous policy responses. In particular, policies for the encouragement of technology transfer have evolved over the years and have been the subject of provisions in IIAs. This paper places such policies in a wider context. As shown in Section I, the encouragement of technology transfer cannot be seen in isolation. It is a policy that is closely related to the broader treatment of proprietary knowledge through intellectual property laws; to the structure of the market, and the conduct of transactions, which may impact on the competitive process in relation to the generation, transfer and dissemination of technology; and to host country measures designed to control the process of technology generation, transfer and diffusion through performance requirements.

In the light of the above, two broad policy approaches to technology issues are identified in Section II. One is a regulatory approach, which, though preserving the essential characteristics of intellectual property rights, seeks to intervene in the market for technology so as to rectify perceived inequalities in that market as between the technology owner and the technology recipient. The latter is seen as the weaker bargaining party. This can be remedied through regulatory intervention in technology transfer transactions, through, for example, the outlawing of provisions in technology transfer transactions that may be seen unduly to favour the technology owner. Coupled with such policies may be a discretion on the part of the receiving country to impose performance requirements on the technology owner as a condition for the transfer transaction to take place. Such policies have, in the past, been adopted by developing host countries and have informed the content of a number of international instruments. These are surveyed in Section II.

A contrasting approach sees the transfer of technology as being best undertaken in a market-based environment. Thus the emphasis is not on regulation or intervention in the technology transfer process, but more on the creation of conditions for a free market transfer of technology. The principal features of this approach are a reliance on the protection of private rights to technology based on intellectual property laws; the absence of direct intervention in the content or conduct of technology transfer transactions, save where these violate principles of competition law by reason of their market-distorting effects and/or by their use of unreasonable restrictive trade practices; and by the prohibition, or highly proscribed use, of technology-related performance requirements. More recent IIAs display such an approach and are also covered in Section II.

Section III considers the interaction of technology transfer issues with other issues covered by IIAs. In particular, there is strong interaction between technology transfer and scope and definition questions, admission and establishment, the most-favoured-nation standard, national treatment and fair and equitable treatment, taxation, environment, host country operational measures, funds transfer and competition.

Section IV concludes by outlining seven possible options concerning the role to be played by provisions on technology in IIAs. These are considered in the light of the market for technology and the position of developing countries therein. The seven options are: no coverage of technology issues; limited coverage of technology issues: control over technology-related performance requirements; limited coverage of technology issues: permissible technology transfer requirements; wide "regulated" coverage of technology issues; wide "market-based" coverage of technology issues; a "hybrid" approach; and the regional industrial policy approach.

INTRODUCTION

The transfer of technology to developing countries has been one of the most discussed areas of international economic relations in the past thirty or more years. In particular, the role of TNCs in the process of developing, applying and disseminating technology across national borders to such countries has generated special interest. One result has been the institution of numerous policy initiatives at the national, regional and multilateral levels. These have, in turn, produced a significant number of legal provisions both in national law and in international instruments. It is the purpose of this paper to analyse the provisions on technology transfer that are found in international instruments, with special focus on IIAs. Technology has always been important to economic well-being; the current technological context makes it critical to development. It is rapidly transforming all productive systems and facilitating international economic integration. An analysis of IIAs and the transfer of technology to developing countries has to take account of this changing context. That is done in the first part of Section I below.

Any discussion of investment by TNCs and technology needs a sound understanding of two basic issues: first what is actually meant by the terms "technology" and "technology transfer" and, secondly, how firms in developing countries actually become proficient in using technology. As to the first, "technology" can be defined in various ways.[1] The present concern is to identify, for legal purposes, a definition that encompasses all forms of commercially usable knowledge, whether patented or unpatented, which can form the subject matter of a transfer transaction. The UNCTAD draft International Code on the Transfer of Technology (the draft TOT Code), in its definition of "technology transfer",[2] describes "technology" as "systematic knowledge for the manufacture of a product, for the application of a process or for the rendering of a service", which Adoes not extend to the transactions involving the mere sale or mere lease of goods" (UNCTAD, 1985, chapter 1, para.1.2.). This definition clearly excludes goods that are sold or hired from the ambit of "technology". Thus it is the knowledge that goes into the creation and provision of the product or service that constitutes "technology", not the finished product or service as such.

Such knowledge should be seen as encompassing both the technical knowledge on which the end product is based, and the organizational capacity to convert the relevant productive inputs into the finished item or service, as the case may be. Consequently, "technology" includes not only "knowledge or methods that are necessary to carry on or to improve the existing production and distribution of goods and services" or indeed to develop entire new products or processes, but also "entrepreneurial expertise and professional know-how" (Santikarn, 1981, p. 4.). The latter two elements may often prove to be the essential competitive advantage possessed by the technology owner.

"Technology transfer" is the process by which commercial technology is disseminated. This takes the form of a technology transfer transaction, which may or may not be covered by a legally binding contract (Blakeney, 1989, p. 136), but which involves the communication, by the transferor, of the relevant knowledge to the recipient. Among the types of transfer transactions that may be used, the draft TOT Code has listed the following:

"(a) The assignment, sale and licensing of all forms of industrial property, except for trade marks, service marks and trade names when they are not part of transfer of technology transactions;

(b) The provision of know-how and technical expertise in the form of feasibility studies, plans, diagrams, models, instructions, guides, formulae, basic or detailed engineering designs, specifications and equipment for training, services involving technical advisory and managerial personnel, and personnel training;

(c) The provision of technological knowledge necessary for the installation, operation and functioning of plant and equipment, and turnkey projects;

(d) The provision of technological knowledge necessary to acquire, install and use machinery, equipment, intermediate goods and/or raw materials which have been acquired by purchase, lease or other means;

(e) The provision of technological contents of industrial and technical co-operation arrangements" (UNCTAD, 1996a, vol. I, p. 183).[3]

  The list excludes non-commercial technology transfers, such as those found in international cooperation agreements between developed and developing countries. Such agreements may relate to infrastructure or agricultural development, or to international cooperation in the fields of research, education, employment or transport (Blakeney, 1989, p. 3). At the outset, technology transfer should be distinguished from technology *diffusion*. The latter is better seen as another benefit that the transfer of technology may bring to a host economy. This can be achieved by the fact that the introduction of a technology into a host country creates an awareness of that technology. That awareness may spill over into the economy as a whole. This may occur without any deliberate intent, simply through the passage of time, or it may occur as a result of deliberate policies on the part of the host country, such as training requirements for local personnel or the compulsory licensing of technology to local firms, or as a result of TNC strategy in the form of purchase of inputs, components and services from local firms, requiring the latter to become familiar with the technology involved so as to be able to perform the functions required by the TNC.

As to the second issue, recent work, including recent reports by UNCTAD, shows why importing and mastering technologies in developing countries is not as easy as earlier assumed (UNCTAD, 1999a and 1998a). At an earlier stage in the debate on technology transfer to developing countries, it was assumed that the main issue to be resolved was the securing of access to new technology. What has become increasingly apparent since that time is that the mere possession of technology does not result in improved technical development or economic gain: the capacity to understand, interact with and learn from that technology is critical. Thus, in the contemporary context, the design of policies must rely on an understanding of the technology development process, the role of TNCs in this process, and their interactions with local learning (UNCTAD, 1999a, pp. 196-197). Furthermore, TNCs play an important role in the generation, transfer and diffusion of technology. This suggests the need to consider the market for technology and the determinants of transfer.

Thus Section I, in explaining the relevant issues, deals, first, with the generation, transfer and diffusion of technology and, secondly, with the main policy issues arising in international rule-making. The paper is selective in dealing with these issues. It does not cover the full range of normative issues related to the generation, transfer and diffusion of technology but rather deals with those issues that relate more strictly to the interface between foreign direct investment (FDI) and technology in the context of IIAs and other relevant instruments. More specifically, the paper deals with the following questions: the treatment of proprietary knowledge; the transfer of technology process; competition issues; and technology-related host-country measures. It does not deal in detail with the increasingly important issue of environmentally sensitive technology; this is given the required fuller coverage in the paper on *Environment* in this Series.

Section II takes stock of the manner in which existing investment instruments have dealt with the main issues identified in Section I. Here some clarification concerning scope is called for. The instruments to be covered include a range of instruments not directly related to FDI. Similar difficulties were faced in the preparation of other papers in the Series, such as *Environment, Employment* and *Social Responsibility*, where the substantive issue goes beyond the narrower questions of the promotion and protection of investors and their investments, and extends to regulatory standards of behaviour for TNCs. Such standards are often to be found in instruments other than IIAs. Hence, to ensure a full and accurate coverage of the relevant provisions that might be of importance to negotiators dealing with technology transfer issues, a wider range of instruments and draft instruments has been examined

Section III considers the interaction with other issues and concepts. Technology transfer as a cross-cutting issue interacts with most of the concepts in the other papers in the Series. However, it has a more relevant interaction with admission and establishment in relation to technology screening procedures, scope and definition, standards of treatment (most-favoured-nation treatment, national treatment and fair and equitable treatment), host country operational measures, taxation, transfer of funds, competition and the environment.

The last section of the paper deals with economic and development implications and policy options with specific focus on how IIAs could enhance the role of FDI in the generation, transfer and diffusion of technology.

Notes

1   See further Blakeney, 1989, pp. 1-2; Santikarn, 1981, pp. 3-6; and Ubezonu, 1990, pp. 24-39.

2   The draft TOT Code definition is used in this paper. Unless otherwise indicated, all instruments cited herein may be found in UNCTAD, 1996a or 2000b.

3   Draft TOT Code, Chapter 1, para.1.3. During negotiations the Group of 77 countries wished to see these as mere examples of technology transfer transactions, while the major developed capital- and technology-exporting states, Group B, and the then socialist Group D, saw them as exhaustive.

Section I

EXPLANATION OF THE ISSUE

As noted in the Introduction, this Section deals, first, with the economic context in which the process of technology transfer through FDI occurs, emphasizing the role of TNCs therein as the main generators, transferors and diffusers of technology. Secondly, it explores the main policy issues resulting from those features, namely the treatment of proprietary knowledge; the regulation of technology transfers; competition issues; and technology-related host-country measures.

A. The role of TNCs in the generation, transfer and diffusion of technology

One of the most important contributions that host developing countries seek from TNCs investing in their economies is technology. This is because a large proportion of the generation of commercially significant technology takes place within TNCs that, accordingly, play a significant role in its transfer and diffusion. Indeed, the international market for technology is dominated by such firms. This has a significant impact on the policy options available for dealing with technology issues in IIAs, as will be further explored in Section IV of this paper. For the present, it is enough to consider the role of FDI undertaken by TNCs in the generation, transfer and diffusion of technology.

1. Technology generation

The impact of FDI on technology generation in developing countries has so far been limited. TNCs tend to centralize their research and development (R&D) facilities in their home countries and a few other industrially advanced countries (UNCTAD, 1999a, pp. 199-202).

On the whole, developing countries continue to attract only marginal portions of foreign affiliate research, and much of what they get relates to adaptation and technical support rather than innovation. Indeed, the majority of developing countries does not have the technological infrastructure to make it economical for TNCs to set up local R&D facilities (UNCTAD, 2000a, pp. 173-174). On the other hand, a number of firms from developing countries are emerging that specialize in niches of opportunity for R&D in such areas as biotechnology, information technology or new areas of services (UNCTAD, 1999a, p. 196), while there are also some instances of TNCs accessing science and technology resources in some developing countries for their R&D activities (Reddy, 2000). Given the greater willingness on the part of TNCs to move their technological assets around the world, such enterprises may offer useful allies for TNCs from both developed and developing countries in the evolution of new technologies.

2. Technology transfer

TNCs are among the main sources of new technology for developing countries. TNCs transfer technologies directly to foreign host countries in two ways: internalized to affiliates under their ownership and control, and externalized to other firms (UNCTAD, 1999a, p. 203). Internalized transfer takes the form of direct investment and is, by definition, the preserve of TNCs. It is difficult to measure and assess directly the amounts of technology transferred in this manner. However, even when measured by payments for royalties and licence fees (a partial measure, since these do not include the cost of technology provided outside of contractual arrangements), a substantial part of technology payments is estimated to be made intra-firm. Furthermore, the trend towards the forging of strategic alliances between competing firms for the development and application of new technologies has created networks within which technology is transferred, and has tended to blur the distinction between internalized and externalized technology transfer.

Externalized modes of transfer by TNCs take a variety of forms: minority joint ventures, franchising, capital goods sales, licences, technical assistance, subcontracting or original equipment-manufacturing arrangements. TNCs are not the only type of firm that can supply technology by some of these means. Purely national firms can also transfer technology through such means. However, TNCs are very important in high-technology areas and in providing entire packages, including not only the technology but also management, marketing and other factors that can make the technology work to its best limits (UNCTAD, 1999a, p. 203).

What determines the mode of technology transfer? This can be answered by reference to a number of variables. The most important of these are the nature of the technology, in that internalized transfer is more likely in highly complex and fast-moving technology areas so that a firm can retain control over its competitive advantage as the developer and owner of the technology in question; the business strategy of the seller, as when he/she decides that establishing an affiliate with the exclusive global mandate to produce a particular product line is the best way to exploit its competitive advantages; the capabilities of the buyer, in that an externalized transfer assumes the existence of a competent licensee, the absence of which may require an internalized transfer to a new affiliate (often at higher cost and risk than licensing to a third party) where projected demand for the product or service involved justifies such expenditure; and host government policies that may stipulate the licensing of technology to local partners as the only permitted mode of TNC participation. These factors are listed more fully in figure I.1.

From a purely commercial perspective, it may be desirable to allow TNCs a "free choice of means" in determining whether to transfer technology internally or externally. However, from a development perspective there may be certain advantages and disadvantages stemming from the choice of transfer mode. Naturally, this discussion assumes the possibility of a choice: where no suitable external recipient exists, an internalized transfer becomes the only feasible way forward. This can occur either through the establishment of a new affiliate in a host country, or through the acquisition of a local firm that can be turned into a suitable recipient (UNCTAD, 2000a, pp. 174-176). Given the existence of a commercially feasible choice, the advantages to development from an internalized transfer include:

Figure I.1. Determinants of the mode of technology transfer

Internalized or externalized technology transfer	Nature of technology	Complexity, speed of change, novelty of technology Degree of centralization needed for R&D Product- or process-based technologies
	Strategy of seller	Size and corporate strategies Concentration on specific product technologies and dependence on brand names Experience of international technology transfer
	Capabilities of buyer	Firm skills and technological capabilities Availability of skills and information in factor markets Institutions supporting skill/technology development
	Host government policies	FDI and intellectual property stance Policies supporting local firms and capabilities FDI bargaining and targeting capabilities

Source: UNCTAD, 1999a, p. 204.

- the provision of financial resources along with technology;
- the possibility of expanding the technological base of the host economy (though this is not exclusive to internalized transfer);
- the use of advanced technology that may not be available through externalized transfer or the use of mature technology applied in an international production network;
- greater speed of transfer:

- access to the technological assets of a TNC providing essential components as well as offering learning opportunities for the host economy.

By contrast, the disadvantages of internalized transfer include:

- The host economy must pay for the entire "package" brought by a TNC which, in addition to technology, may include brand names, finance, skills and management. Internalized transfer may prove more expensive than externalization, especially where local firms already possess these other components of the package.
- The retention of technology and skills within the network of a TNC may hold back deeper learning processes and spillovers into the local economy, especially where the local affiliate is not developing R&D capabilities.

Thus, where a choice exists between internal transfers to foreign affiliates or external transfers to local technology recipients, governments may wish to intervene to affect the terms of transfer associated with each modality, as, for example, where incentives are offered to TNCs for the transfer of advanced technical functions. Another approach is to upgrade the capacity of the host economy to receive and benefit from technology transfer (UNCTAD, 1999a, p. 210).

3. Technology diffusion

The use of new technology by a recipient is only one of its benefits that the recipient's economy obtains from that technology. Another, often larger, benefit is the diffusion of technology and skills within the host economy. Many forms of diffusion are not priced or paid for in markets. They are externalities that arise involuntarily or are deliberately undertaken to overcome information problems. Thus,

=> Eg of IT externality

in response to the presence of TNCs, local firms and industries may become linked into the technological processes of those firms through "demonstration effects", as where domestic firms seek to imitate the technology applied by TNCs, and to compete with TNCs by improving their technological capabilities and raising productivity. Even more importantly, diffusion can occur through cooperation between foreign affiliates and domestic suppliers and customers, leading to technology transfer to vertically linked firms and service providers (UNCTAD, 2001a). Furthermore, labour mobility from foreign affiliates to domestic firms, particularly of highly skilled personnel, can stimulate technological development.

On the other hand, such spillover effects may not be inevitable, as where a TNC closely guards its competitive advantage in its technology, whether through its retention within the TNC network, and/or through limited skills transfer to employees and/or through restrictive terms in employee contracts, preventing them from revealing technical secrets or from working for direct competitors for a set period of time.

B. Main policy issues

In the light of the above, what are the main issues that arise in relation to the generation, transfer and diffusion of technology in a host country?   To answer this question, one needs to consider the type of policy measures used by Governments to influence technology development. In the first place, the generation, transfer and diffusion of technology should not be seen as a linear process: in practice, each of these phases influences the others in a multidirectional way.

Secondly, at the domestic level, countries have used a variety of policy instruments to influence and strengthen the generation, transfer and diffusion of technology (Omer, 2001).   These policy instruments included regimes for the protection of intellectual property rights (IPRs), competition laws, performance requirements (e.g. joint venture and local R&D requirements) and a variety of promotion instruments (e.g. fiscal and financial incentives, training facilities). Furthermore, certain developing countries, notably in Latin America, experimented during the 1970s with specialized technology transfer laws, whose aim was to regulate the content of technology licensing agreements with a view to ensuring that the development objectives of a host country economy would not be undermined by unequal terms in technology transfer transactions.

At the international level, and particularly in the context of IIAs, the following policy issues can be discerned: the treatment of proprietary knowledge; encouraging technology transfer; competition and technology transfer; and technology-related host-country measures. The paper thus focuses on these issues. It should be noted that, just as the processes of generation, transfer and diffusion of technology are interrelated issues, the policy issues that have dominated IIAs should be seen as interrelated as well. For example, it was the acceptance of the proprietary nature of technology, particularly as regards patentable knowledge, by TNCs and their home governments that was at the heart of the debates on the content of a new regime for the transfer of technology to developing countries under the draft TOT Code. The developing countries questioned this assumption and put forward the alternative view that technology was in the nature of a necessary public good in relation to the development of less developed countries and that, therefore, some of the private property related assumptions of the international system for the protection of intellectual property should be amended in the interests of developing countries (Muchlinski, 1999, pp. 438-444). The intention was not to alter the existing arrangements on IPRs as such, in that the draft TOT Code encouraged each country adopting legislation on the protection of IPRs to ensure that these be effectively protected. Rather, it was to make certain that the terms of a technology transfer agreement were not of a kind that would effectively prevent a recipient in a developing host country from the unrestricted use of the technology, and its attendant know-how, after the expiry of the agreement and that host developing countries would be free to pursue their industrial policies as they saw fit, including, where deemed necessary, through the imposition of performance requirements upon technology transferors (Roffe and Tesfachew, 2001, p. 389).

1. Treatment of proprietary knowledge

IPR regimes have been the classical policy instruments to influence the generation, transfer and diffusion of technology and international rule-making has preponderantly focused on the protection of IPRs. International rule-making in this field has a long-standing tradition (Blakeney, 1989). It has mainly centred on avoiding or lessening the consequences arising from disparities among domestic intellectual property laws as to the formal and substantial requirements of protection through basic principles aimed at:

- avoiding discrimination towards foreigners as regards IPR protection; and
- attenuating the territorial character of IPRs which obliges enterprises willing to expand operations to foreign countries to seek protection in each of them on the basis of differing formal and substantive requirements and procedures.

The protection of IPRs was not traditionally linked to the operation of foreign firms in a host country. Advocates of stronger IPRs hold that increased protection together with adequate enforcement mechanisms would increase FDI flows and associated technology transfer to developing countries (Beier, 1980). However, empirical evidence on this is rather mixed. Some authors suggest that stronger IPRs are likely to have a positive impact on FDI while others are more cautious (see Minta, 1990, p. 43; UNTCMD, 1993;

Ferrantino, 1993; Kondo, 1995; Mansfield, 1994 and 1995; Maskus and Yang, 2000).

Due to the increasing importance of technological assets as a source of competitive advantage for TNCs, IPR protection has been incorporated into the multilateral trading system. The TRIPS Agreement is perhaps the most prominent example of such incorporation. In relation to IIAs, the treatment of proprietary knowledge raises the following main issues:

- the link between protection of IPRs and FDI flows;
- enforcement of IPRs;
- the issue of exhaustion and parallel imports;
- compulsory licensing.

The first of these issues asserts that, in order to stimulate the flow of inward FDI, a host country must ensure the protection of the foreign investors' competitive advantage by offering legal protection of the IPRs by which that advantage is obtained. Thus the first aim of any international regime must be to ensure that mutual recognition and protection of IPRs exist. That entails the second issue, how IPRs are to be enforced. Here the major concern is to ensure that IPRs have equivalent protection in all jurisdictions in which an owner uses those rights. Turning to the third issue, the principle of exhaustion as applied in Europe, and its equivalent in the United States, the first sale doctrine, were developed to circumscribe the scope of the exclusive rights granted to title-holders. Thus, according to this principle, which was developed mainly through case law in different jurisdictions, once owners of IPRs (whether a patent, trademark, copyright or design) have placed protected products on the market, they are no longer entitled to control the subsequent marketing stages of those products, beyond what might be legitimately required to protect the subject-matter of the rights. The aim of this principle is to prevent the abuse of the monopoly over the first placement of a protected product or process enjoyed by an IPR owner by means of the prevention of parallel trade in that product or process by third parties. This may occur, for example, where owners use their IPRs to prevent third parties from trading freely in a given product even though they had acquired it legitimately in the course of their business, especially where they had been granted the right to use the IPRs concerned by way of a licence from the owners, or where the goods were acquired in a jurisdiction where no IPR protection for those goods had been recognized and the goods had been freely placed on that market by the IPR owners.

As regards compulsory licensing, this involves an authorization to exploit an invention given by a public authority, in specific cases defined by law. The aim is to prevent IPR owners from preventing third parties from gaining access to those goods or technology by relying on their exclusive rights over the IPRs in question. The effect might be to deprive consumers and the economy in general of the possibility of benefiting from the exploitation of the protected goods or technology, to the detriment of economic welfare and technical progress. This issue could also be seen in the context of competition as discussed in the relevant Section below.

2. Encouraging technology transfer

The encouragement of technology transfer to developing countries has been a recurrent issue on the international economic agenda of the past three decades. The draft UNCTAD Code of Conduct on the Transfer of Technology addressed the issue from various perspectives: the legitimization of specific domestic policies to promote the transfer and diffusion of technology; rules governing the contractual conditions of transfer of technology transactions; special measures on differential treatment for developing countries; and measures that would strengthen international cooperation.[1] The approach was to concentrate on the supply side of the market and to remedy constraints on the acquisition of technology by developing countries caused by the domination of the international technology market by TNCs. In particular, it was proposed to liberalize trade in technology and to introduce guidelines on the terms and conditions of transfer of technology to developing countries. This approach concentrated on the transfer of technology per se, rather than on its diffusion. However, as will be discussed further in the next subsection, this approach has been overtaken by other developments, mainly in relation to the enhancement of competition in the transfer of technology.

More recently the transfer of environmentally sound technologies has been added to the agenda of IIAs in the context of technology transfer. One of the results of recent international agreements on environmental matters has been a greater emphasis on the need for TNCs to ensure that the technology they transfer to developing countries in particular is conducive to good environmental management. This is to be achieved not only through the transfer of environmentally sound technologies, but also through the transfer of environmentally sound management practices. These aspects of technology transfer are more fully discussed in the paper on *Environment* in this Series (UNCTAD, 2001b).

At a more general level, one of the main policy issues facing developing countries in the era of globalization and liberalization is to determine how far they can go in adopting market-oriented strategies in order to attract FDI and ensure economic growth, and at the same time assess the extent of the limitations that need to be applied to such strategies if damage is not to be done to their economies in the short to medium term. Transfer of technology is a microcosmic reflection of this larger issue. Most developing countries, despite strenuous efforts, remain net consumers rather than producers of technology. They still pay more in royalties and licence fees than they earn from their efforts to attract technology. Thus finding the right balance is the crux of the matter.

3. Competition-related questions

As pointed out above, earlier attempts at the multilateral regulation of technology transfer concentrated on defensive measures that could remedy dysfunctions in the international market for technology or influence the functioning of the market with a view to better achieving development goals. Today, however, defensive measures are less in favour on the grounds that market imperfections are best addressed by measures aimed at improving the contestability of such markets. Hence competition policy acquires a greater significance vis-à-vis market interventions that seek to modulate in a mandatory manner the conditions under which technology transfer takes place (UNCTAD, 1999a, p. 222).

The main interface between the generation, transfer and diffusion of technology and competition law relates to the control of restrictive business practices in licensing agreements - one of the major objectives of the draft TOT Code. The abandonment of the draft TOT Code was due to the then continuing disagreement between developing and developed country models of technology transfer regulation. The former wished to take an economic regulation oriented approach which concentrated on the review of clauses in technology licensing agreements with a view to the prohibition of those clauses seen as inimical to the development process and/or likely to take advantage of the weaker bargaining position of the local technology recipient. The latter saw the issue primarily as one of ensuring effective competition in the transfer of technology and, accordingly, held the view that only those clauses that could be seen as unreasonable restrictions on the freedom of the recipient to compete, or which placed unreasonable restraints on the competitive freedom of third parties, would be regulated. These two policy goals do not necessarily produce the same results. For example, a reasonable tie-in clause might be acceptable on a competition-based analysis, but may be seen as a barrier to the development of local supply chains in the context of a developing country economy (Muchlinski, 1999, pp. 433-436).

Much of this debate has now been overtaken by the orientation of the TRIPS agreement. The new rules that it has introduced, which follow the competition-oriented model of technology transfer regulation, have made many instruments used in the past by the then newly industrializing countries difficult to apply (UNCTAD, 1999a, p. 223). Specialized technology transfer laws are perhaps the best example here. On the other hand, there is scope for competitiveness-oriented strategies to be adopted by developing countries to improve their ability to assimilate and develop technology (UNCTAD, 1999a, pp. 223-228; UNCTAD, 2001a).

4. Technology-related host-country measures

Once admitted into a country, foreign firms are subject to the host country's jurisdiction. Thus, industrial policies have traditionally been within the regulatory domain of the host country. Governments still retain a space to adopt industrial policies to attract FDI and to increase its benefit to the host economy. However, as has been pointed out in other papers in this Series, the legal regulation of FDI is now increasingly accepted as a matter of international concern.

Recent years have seen the emergence of limitations imposed upon host countries by international agreements as to the form in which some domestic policies are applied. In this regard, certain host country operational measures, aimed at inducing foreign investors to adopt a more active approach towards the transfer and dissemination of technology, may no longer be capable of being adopted by countries that have acceded to international instruments containing such limitations. This matter is given full coverage in the paper on *Host Country Operational Measures* in this Series (UNCTAD, 2001d).

In terms of subject-matter, the following technology-related host-country measures may have an impact on the pace and direction of technology transfer to and dissemination in a developing host country:

- restrictions on employment of foreign professional and technical personnel, and requirements concerning the training of local personnel;
- transfer of technology requirements;
- restrictions on royalty payments;
- R&D requirements.

Each type of requirement aims to alter the conditions under which investors apply their technological capabilities in a host country context. Thus an investor may be required to limit the number of foreign professional and technical personnel and increase the number of local personnel who can be trained up to international standards. Equally, a host country may require that specific types of technology, seen as being of importance to the host economy in general and/or to the industry concerned, are transferred to the host country by a foreign investor. Furthermore, the level of royalty that is charged by a foreign investor for the transfer of the technology in question, whether to an affiliate or third-party recipient, may be subjected to scrutiny to ensure that the consideration that is being paid for access to that technology is reasonable. Finally, a host country may require that a foreign investor establishes a level of R&D activity in the host county so as to develop the technology in question in accordance with local needs and/or so as to offer higher value-added activities in the host country associated with the presence of that technology. As noted above, whether such measures can be taken by a host country now depends on the nature and content of that country's international commitments regarding the imposition of performance requirements upon foreign investors.

Note

1   For a review of the origins and aftermath of the draft TOT Code, see Patel et al., 2001, especially the chapter by Roffe and Tesfachew; and UNCTAD, 1999a, p. 222, box VII.10.

Section II

STOCKTAKING AND ANALYSIS

This section of the paper takes stock of the manner in which investment-related instruments have dealt with the main issues identified in Section I. As noted in Section I, given the nature of this topic not only IIAs but also other international instruments, notably international IPR conventions, are examined.

A. Treatment of proprietary knowledge

1. The relationship between IPR protection and FDI flows

The importance of IPRs for the stimulation of investment flows is exemplified at the outset of an IIA where the definition provisions include such rights within the definition of "investments" to which the protective provisions of the agreement apply. This matter has been raised in the paper on *Scope and Definition* in this Series (UNCTAD, 1999b, pp. 20-21). It will be further discussed in Section III below.

A further factor to bear in mind is that, where an IIA refers to the national laws and regulations of a host country, these include its IPR laws. Thus, in the case of bilateral investment treaties (BITs), other than those concluded by the United States and Canada, it is common to include a provision making the entry and establishment of an investor and/or investment from the other contracting party subject to the laws and regulations in force in the receiving contracting party (UNCTAD, 1998b, pp. 46-50). Where such laws include IPR laws, then the investor/ investment is subject to any regulatory requirements contained in these laws. The resulting effect on FDI flows depends on the content of these laws.

In this regard the content of IPR conventions becomes significant. These instruments prescribe the main principles upon which the interaction of national IPR laws with foreign investors, who enjoy IPRs recognized under the laws of another country, should be conducted. The core principles to be found in the main international IPR conventions are summarized in box II 1.

Box II.1. Main IPR principles in major international conventions

National treatment (Rome Convention, Article 2.1; Paris Convention, Article 2)

Right of priority (Paris Convention, Article 4)

Independence of patents obtained for the same invention in different countries (Paris Convention, Article 4bis)

Right to take legislative measures for the grant of compulsory licences (Paris Convention, Article 5)

Special provisions regarding developing countries (Berne Convention, Appendix)

Source: UNCTAD.

What the content of international IPR conventions should be is a matter that has generated controversy over the years. In particular, the developing countries have not always been content to accept the major principles of IPR protection enshrined in conventions elaborated and subscribed to by the developed countries (Blakeney, 1989; Roffe, 2000). Furthermore, the presence of heightened IPR protection may not provide a clear impetus to FDI flows (UNTCMD, 1993; Roffe, 2000, p. 411). Nonetheless, the TRIPS Agreement, which is regarded as the current benchmark paradigm of international IPR protection (Roffe, 2000, p. 408),[1] provides in Article 7:

"*Objectives.*

The protection and enforcement of intellectual property rights should contribute to the promotion of technological innovation and to the transfer and dissemination of technology, to the mutual advantage of producers and users of technological knowledge and in a manner conducive to social and economic welfare, and to a balance of rights and obligations" (UNCTAD, 1996a, vol. I., pp. 341-342).

This represents a clear endorsement of the beneficial effects of IPR protection for economic welfare. It should be read in the light of Article 8 of the TRIPS Agreement:

"*Principles.*

1. Members may, in formulating or amending their laws and regulations, adopt measures necessary to protect public health and nutrition, and to promote the public interest in sectors of vital importance to their socio-economic and technological development, provided that such measures are consistent with the provisions of this agreement.
2. Appropriate measures, provided that they are consistent with the provisions of this Agreement, may be needed to prevent the abuse of intellectual property rights by right holders or the resort to practices which unreasonably restrain trade or adversely affect the international transfer of technology" (UNCTAD, 1996a, vol. I., p. 342).

A broad, purposive interpretation of these two provisions suggests that members have, as a matter of principle, considerable discretion to impose competition policy and technology transfer related measures on foreign patent holders, provided the overall level of IPR protection conforms to that provided in the TRIPS Agreement (Trebilcock and Howse, 1999, pp. 322-323). However, it is not clear from these provisions how the protection of IPRs is to contribute to the transfer of technology to developing countries. Unless these provisions are construed as imposing some obligation on the part of technology-exporting countries, they will offer little more than aspirational hopes for developing countries. These issues are further considered in the light of TRIPS provisions, and provisions in other international instruments, in the ensuing subsections.

With regard to the basic standards that members of TRIPS are required to meet, these revolve around national treatment in Article 3 and most-favoured-nation treatment in Article 4. These obligations do not apply to procedures provided in multilateral agreements concluded under the auspices of the World Intellectual Property Organisation (WIPO) relating to the maintenance and acquisition of IPRs (see TRIPS Agreement, Article 5, in UNCTAD, 1996a, vol. I, p. 341). Furthermore, the members= obligations under TRIPS, in relation to standards concerning the availability, scope and use of IPRs (Part II), enforcement (Part III) and acquisition and maintenance of IPRs and related *inter partes* procedures (Part IV), are subject to their obligations to comply with Articles 1 to 12 and Article 19 of the Paris Convention (1967), and nothing in the TRIPS Agreement may be read as derogating from the members existing obligations to each other under the Paris Convention, the Berne Convention, the Rome Convention and the Treaty on Intellectual Property in Respect of Integrated Circuits (see TRIPS Agreement, Article 2, in UNCTAD, 1996a, vol. I, p. 340). The substantive protection offered to IPR owners by the TRIPS Agreement is summarized in box II.2.

It should be noted that these obligations do not automatically apply to developing countries. Thus, while by virtue of Article 65(1) of the TRIPS Agreement, all members are entitled not to apply the Agreement before the expiration of one year from the entry into force of the WTO Agreement, Article 65(2) gives a developing country a further period of four years following the general transition period applicable to all members under paragraph 1. Thus, developing countries are entitled not to apply the Agreement for a period of five years after the entry into force of the WTO Agreement. Since the latter Agreement entered into force in 1995, the transitional period for developing countries expired in 2000. A developing country may also delay the application of the product patent protection provisions of the Agreement for a further five years where such protection extends to areas of technology that are not currently protectable in that country's territory. Under Article 66 (1) of the TRIPS Agreement, the least developed country members are exempted for ten years from the date of general application of the Agreement set out in paragraph 1, i.e. 11 years after the entry into force of the WTO Agreement. In addition, they may apply for further extensions of that exemption (UNCTAD, 1996a, vol. I, p. 368).

Box II.2. IPR protection in the TRIPS Agreement

The TRIPS Agreement sets standards relating to the protection of patents, copyright and related rights, trademarks and geographical indications, trade secrets and confidential information, integrated circuit design, and industrial design, and covers both substantive standards and specific issues of enforcement that are generally applicable to these. The following provisions are noteworthy:

Patents:
* Member States may not exclude any field of technology from patentability as a whole, and they may not discriminate as to the place of invention when rights are granted (Article 27).
* Domestic patent laws must provide a minimum term of 20 years of protection from the filing date. Such protection must depend on uniform conditions of eligibility, and specified exclusive rights must be granted (Article 33).
* The patentees' exclusive rights must include the right to supply the market with imports of the patented products (Article 28).
* Compulsory licensing remains available and can be granted under the existing law of a member country, subject to the conditions set forth in the Agreement (Article 31).

/...

(Box II.2, continued)

Copyright and related rights:
- Protection of works covered by the Berne Convention, excluding moral rights, with respect to expression and not the ideas, procedures, methods of operation or mathematical concepts as such (Article 9).
- Protection of computer programmes as literary works and compilations of data (Article 10).
- Recognition of rental rights, at least for phonograms, computer programmes and cinematographic works (except if rental has not led to widespread copying that impairs the reproduction rights) (Article 11).
- Recognition of rights of performers, producers of phonograms and broadcasting organizations (Article 14).

Trademarks and geographical indications:
- Strengthens several aspects of trademark law, including strengthening protection of service-marks and of well-known marks.
- Geographical indications are subject to the general principles (Part I) and to the provisions of enforcement (Part II).

Trade secrets and confidential information:
- Countries are required to protect information that is commercially valuable, secret and subject to measures to prevent unauthorized disclosure against unfair commercial practices.
- Countries must also protect secret data submitted to government authorities in connection with applications for the approval of pharmaceutical and agrochemical products.

Integrated circuit design:
- Mandates compliance with core substantive provisions of the Treaty on Intellectual Property in Respect of Integrated Circuits of 1989 (Washington Treaty) (which is not yet in force). These provisions obliged WTO members to prohibit unauthorized imports, sales or commercial distribution of a protected layout design of an integrated circuit embodying such a design, or of an article incorporating an integrated circuit, for at least ten years, subject to a good faith exception.

/...

2. Enforcement of IPRs

Part III of the TRIPS Agreement contains a comprehensive section on enforcement obligations and procedures. In particular, under Article 41, members must:

"•   Ensure that effective enforcement procedures are available under their law against any act of infringement of IPRs covered by this Agreement, including expeditious remedies to prevent infringements and deterrent remedies to prevent further infringements.

*   Apply such procedures in a manner that avoids the creation of barriers to trade.

*   Provide procedures that are fair and equitable, not unnecessarily complicated or costly, or entailing unreasonable time-limits or delays.

*   Decisions should be reasoned and in writing, and available to the parties and will be based only on evidence in respect of which the parties were offered an opportunity to be heard.

(Box II.2, concluded)

Industrial design:
*   Participating States are relatively free to draft domestic design protection laws with local objectives in mind. Although members must provide some form of design protection to satisfy both the TRIPS Agreement provisions and the Paris Convention (Article 5 quinquies), countries may resort either to an industrial property law or to copyright law for these purposes, and they need not protect fundamentally determined designs at all.
*   Members must protect textile designs, however, either in a design law or in copyright law, and if *sui generis* laws are adopted for this or other purposes, they must protect appearance design against copying for at least a ten-year period.

Source: UNCTAD, 1996b.

• Decisions must be subject to judicial review" (UNCTAD, 1996a, vol. I, pp. 357-358).

These general principles are further elaborated in Articles 42-61 of the TRIPS Agreement. The provisions in Part III of the TRIPS Agreement offer a significant inroad into domestic civil and administrative procedures (Trebilcock and Howse, 1999, p. 327). However Article 41(5) makes clear that this Part does not "create any obligation to put in place a judicial system for the enforcement of intellectual property rights distinct from that for the enforcement of law in general, nor does it affect the capacity of the Members to enforce their law in general. Nothing in this Part creates any obligation with respect to the distribution of resources as between enforcement of intellectual property rights and the enforcement of law in general" (ibid.).

3. Exhaustion of IPRs and parallel imports

The TRIPS Agreement, Article 6, deals briefly with the issue of exhaustion, stating that, "[f]or the purposes of dispute settlement under this Agreement, subject to the provisions of Articles 3 and 4 nothing in this Agreement shall be used to address the issue of the exhaustion of intellectual property rights". This provision is the result of a compromise. Traditionally each country has established its own policy on the treatment of parallel imports. During the Uruguay Round negotiations it was found to be impossible to agree on a global standard for national exhaustion of IPRs. Thus, Article 6 restricts any challenge to the treatment of parallel imports to violations of national treatment (Article 3) and most-favoured-nation treatment (Article 4) (Maskus, 2000, pp. 208-216). Equally, the text of the draft Multilateral Agreement on Investment (MAI) was inconclusive. There was no agreement on whether there needed to be any language on this issue to ensure that the MAI did not create new obligations in this area (UNCTAD, 2000b, vol. IV, p. 145; and UNCTAD, 1999c).

On the other hand, regional economic agreements do deal with the doctrine of exhaustion and the treatment of parallel imports. For example, the Protocol of Harmonization of Norms of Intellectual Property in MERCOSUR on Matters of Trademarks, Geographical Indications and Denominations of Origin (Decision No 8/95) states in Article 13:

> "The registration of a trademark shall not prevent the free circulation of the trademarked products, legally introduced into commerce by the owner or with his authorization. The Party States oblige themselves to include in their respective legislation measures that provide for the exhaustion of the right granted by the registration" (NLC, 1998).

This provision allows for a regional exhaustion of trademarks registered in MERCOSUR member countries. However, it does not create an international exhaustion regime. Thus parallel imports into MERCOSUR of a trademarked product that is marketed outside the region by or with the consent of the registered holder of the trademark may be prevented (Haines Ferrari, 2000, p. 30). This approach echoes the European Union (EU) doctrine of exhaustion of rights, which allows for parallel imports from other EU member States but does not extend this principle to imports from outside the EU.[2]

Decision 486 (2000) of the Andean Community also contains an exhaustion principle. Thus, under Article 54 thereof:

> "A patent shall not confer on its owner the right to proceed against a third party making commercial use of a product protected by a patent once that product has been introduced into the commerce of any country by the owner or another person authorized by the right holder or with economic ties to that patent owner.

For the purposes of the preceding paragraph, two persons shall be considered to have economic ties when one of the persons is able to exercise a decisive influence on the other, either directly or indirectly, with respect to the exploitation of the patent or when a third party is able to exert that influence over both persons."

Article 54 goes on to assert that where a patent protects biological material that is capable of being reproduced, the patent coverage shall not extend to the biological material that is obtained by means of the reproduction, multiplication or propagation of the material that was introduced into the commerce as described in the first paragraph, provided that it was necessary to reproduce, multiply or propagate the material in order to fulfil the purposes for which it was introduced into commerce and that the material so obtained is not used for multiplication or propagation purposes. Finally, Article 55 makes clear that:

"Without prejudice to the provisions stipulated in this Decision with respect to patent nullity, the rights conferred by a patent may not be asserted against a third party that, in good faith and before the priority date or the filing date of the application on which the patent was granted, was already using or exploiting the invention, or had already made effective and serious preparations for such use or exploitation.

In such case, the said third party shall have the right to start or continue using or exploiting the invention, but that right may only be assigned or transferred together with the business or company in which that use or exploitation is taking place."

The principle of exhaustion is extended to other IPRs by Decision 486. Thus Article 131 states that:

"registration of an industrial design shall not confer the right to proceed against a third party who makes commercial use of a product incorporating or reproducing the design once it has been introduced into the commerce of any country by the right holders or another person authorized by them or with economic ties to those right holders."

Article 131 continues by repeating, in relation to industrial designs, the definition of "economic ties" found in Article 54 in the case of patents. In relation to trademarks Article 158 states:

"Trademark registration shall not confer on the owner the rights to prevent third parties from engaging in trade in a product protected by registration once the owner of the registered trademark or another party with the consent of or economic ties to that owner has introduced that product into the trade of any country, in particular where any such products, packaging or packing as may have been in direct contact with the product concerned have not undergone any change, alteration, or deterioration.

For the purposes of the preceding paragraph, two persons shall be considered to have economic ties when one of the persons is able to exercise a decisive influence over the other, either directly or indirectly, with respect to use of the trademark right or when a third party is able to exert that influence over both persons."

Two general observations may be made as regards the content of these provisions. First, the reference to "any country" suggests that the Andean Community recognizes an international exhaustion principle, as the usual qualification restricting the principle to imports from other member countries is absent. Furthermore, the reference to "economic ties" connotes recent developments in the EU doctrine of exhaustion as interpreted by the European Court of Justice in relation to the exhaustion of trademarks, where the economic ties between entities in different countries were considered to be of importance when determining whether the protected product had been placed on the market in the country of export with the consent of the IPR owner.[3]

4. Compulsory licensing

This issue is dealt with in major IPR conventions (Paris Convention). Thus Article 5.A of the Paris Convention provides that where a patent is considered to have been insufficiently worked within a country, within a specified time, that patent may be compulsorily acquired or compulsorily licensed to another enterprise. This aims to prevent an anti-competitive hoarding of patents (Blakeney, 1989, p. 16). Compulsory licensing is also covered in the TRIPS Agreement. Article 31 deals with the compulsory licensing of patents (UNCTAD, 1996a, vol. I, p. 352). This places certain conditions upon the granting of a compulsory licence. Of these, the most significant are:

(i)   Each case will be considered on its individual merits.

(ii)   The proposed user must have made efforts, prior to such use, to obtain authorization from the right holder on reasonable commercial terms and conditions and such efforts have not been successful within a reasonable period of time. This requirement is subject to waiver in case of national emergency or public non-commercial use.

(iii)   The scope and duration of such use will be limited to the purpose for which it was authorized.

(iv)   Such use will be non-exclusive and non-assignable.

(v)   It shall be authorized predominantly for the supply of the domestic market of the member authorizing such use.

(vi)   The authorization will be liable to be terminated if and when the circumstances which led to it cease to exist and are unlikely to recur. This is subject to the adequate protection of the legitimate interests of the persons so authorized.

(vii) The right holder will be paid adequate remuneration.

(viii) Decisions will be subject to judicial review.

Conditions (ii) and (v) may not apply where the use is permitted to remedy any anti-competitive practices (UNCTAD, 1996a, vol. I, p. 352).

Similar requirements can be found in NAFTA, which deals with the issue in Article 1709(10) (NAFTA, 1993, p. 674). The draft MAI indirectly referred to this matter in connection with expropriation issues. It was agreed that text was needed to ensure that certain IPR management and legal provisions did not constitute expropriation (UNCTAD, 2000b, vol. IV, p. 143).

A significant recent statement of the principles surrounding compulsory licensing can be found in Decision 486 (2000) of the Andean Community. The relevant provisions are reproduced in box II.3. The approach largely follows the matters contained in the TRIPS provision, though in somewhat more detail, explicable by the fact that this Decision aims to offer a framework in which the member countries can act on the issue.

In contrast to the above examples from multilateral and regional instruments, BITs are usually silent on the matter of compulsory licensing. However, where a BIT includes IPRs in its definition of protected investments, and where it covers not only direct but also indirect expropriations, the protection offered by the agreement may in itself be enough to cover compulsory licensing in the exceptional case where it can be shown that this has an expropriatory purpose and is carried out in breach of the protective standards of treatment contained in the BIT and in disregard of the relevant provisions of IPR agreements.

Box II.3. Andean Community Decision 486 (2000)

"CHAPTER VII
On the Regime of Compulsory Licensing

Article 61.- At the expiry of a period of three years following a patent grant or of four years following the application for a patent, whichever is longer, the competent national office may grant a compulsory license mainly for the industrial manufacture of the product covered by the patent, or for full use of the patented process, at the request of any interested party, but only if, at the time of the request, the patent had not been exploited in the manner specified in articles 59 and 60, in the Member Country in which the license is sought, or if the exploitation of the invention had been suspended for more than one year.

Compulsory licenses shall not be granted if patent owners are able to give valid reasons for their failure to act, which may be reasons of force majeure or an act of God, in accordance with the domestic provisions in effect in each Member Country.

A compulsory license shall be granted only if, prior to applying for it, the proposed user has made efforts to obtain a contractual license from the patent holder on reasonable commercial terms and conditions and that such efforts were not successful within a reasonable period of time.

Article 62.- Decisions to grant a compulsory license, as stipulated in the previous article, shall be taken after the patent owners have been notified to present their arguments as they see fit within the following sixty days.

The competent national office shall specify the scope or coverage of the license, and in particular shall specify the period for which it is granted, the subject matter of the license, the amount of the remuneration, and the conditions for the payment thereof. The remuneration shall be set at an adequate level in accordance with the individual circumstances of each case and, in particular, the economic value of the authorization.

/...

(Box II.3, continued)

Opposition to a compulsory license shall not prevent its exploitation or have any effect on any periods that may be running. The filing of an objection shall not prevent the patent owner, in the meantime, from collecting the remuneration specified by the competent national office on the part unaffected by the objection.

Article 63.- At the request of the owner of the patent or the licensee, the conditions governing the compulsory license may be changed by the competent national office where new circumstances so dictate and, in particular, when the patent holder grants another license on terms that are more favorable than the existing ones.

Article 64.- The licensee shall exploit the licensed invention within a period of two years following the date the license was granted, unless that licensee is able to give valid reasons for inaction consisting of force majeure or an act of God. Otherwise, at the patent owner's request, the competent national office shall revoke the compulsory license.

Article 65.- Following the declaration by a Member Country of the existence of public interest, an emergency, or national security considerations, and only for so long as those considerations exist, the patent may be subject to compulsory licensing at any time. In that case, the competent national office shall grant the licenses that are applied for. The owner of the patent so licensed shall be notified as soon as is reasonably possible.

The competent national office shall specify the scope or extent of the compulsory license and, in particular, the term for which it is granted, the subject matter of the license, and the amount of remuneration and the conditions for its payment.

The grant of a compulsory license for reasons of public interest shall not reduce the right of the patent owner to continue exploiting it.

/...

(Box II.3, continued)

Article 66.- The competent national office may, either ex officio or at the request of a party, and after having obtained the consent of the national antitrust authority, grant compulsory licenses where practices are noted that are detrimental to the exercise of free competition, especially where they constitute an abuse by the patent owner of a dominant position in the market.

The need to correct anti-competitive practices shall be taken into account in determining the amount of remuneration to be paid in such cases.

The competent national office shall refuse termination of a compulsory license if and when the conditions which led to the granting of the license are likely to recur.

Article 67.- The competent national office shall grant a license, upon request by the owner of a patent whose exploitation necessarily requires the use of another patent, and that right holder has been unable to secure a contractual license to the other patent on reasonable commercial terms. That license shall, without prejudice to the provisions of article 68, be subject to the following conditions:

a) the invention claimed in the second patent shall involve an important technical advance of considerable economic significance in relation to the invention claimed in the first patent;

b) the owner of the first patent shall be entitled to a cross-license on reasonable terms to use the invention claimed in the second patent; and,

c) the license authorized in respect of the first patent shall be non-assignable except with the assignment of the second patent.

/...

(Box II.3, concluded)

Article 68.- In addition to the conditions provided for in the preceding articles, compulsory licenses shall be subject to the following:

a) they shall be non-exclusive and may not be sublicensed;

b) they shall be non-assignable, except with the part of the business or goodwill which permits its industrial use. This shall be evidenced in writing and registered with the competent national office. Otherwise, those assignments or transfers shall not be legally binding;

c) they shall be liable, subject to adequate protection of the legitimate interests of the persons so authorized, to be terminated if and when the circumstances which led to them cease to exist and are unlikely to recur;

d) their scope and duration shall be limited to the purposes for which they were authorized;

e) in the case of patents protecting semi-conductor technology, a compulsory license shall be authorized only for public non-commercial use or to remedy a practice declared by the competent national authority to be anti-competitive in accordance with articles 65 and 66;

f) they provide for payment of adequate remuneration according to the circumstances of each case, taking into account the economic value of the license, without prejudice to the stipulations of article 66; and,

g) they shall be used predominantly for the supply of the domestic market.

Article 69.- Compulsory licenses that fail to comply with the provisions of this Chapter shall be devoid of any legal effect whatsoever."

Source: www.sice.oas.org.

B. Encouraging transfer of technology

This area has seen some significant changes in the approach of international instruments that deal with technology transfer. At least three major approaches can be discerned. The first can be termed the "regulatory" approach. This seeks to encourage increased transfer of technology through collaboration between, in particular, developed and developing countries. It centres on the potentially unequal nature of a technology transfer transaction, especially where the recipient is an enterprise in a developing country. The underlying rationale for provisions displaying this approach is to control the potentially adverse economic consequences of such transfers for the weaker party, which include both the licensee in an external transfer and the developing host country in the case of all transfers. Hence the major features of such provisions include the protection of a host country's internal regulations on technology transfer and the outright prohibition of certain terms in technology transfer transactions that are detrimental to development goals.

The second approach may be termed the "market-based development" approach. Here the technology transfer transaction is not necessarily seen as one between unequal parties. Rather, the private property character of the technology is stressed and a TNC that (in most of these cases) owns the technology is seen as being free to transfer it by whatever means it sees fit. However, given the potential inequality of market power between the owner and recipient of the technology, this freedom for a TNC is subject to certain obligations not to abuse its market power, whether in the case of an external transfer to a licensee or in the course of internal transfers within the TNC network. This matter is considered in the next subsection as it is of sufficient importance to warrant separate and more detailed treatment.

In addition, this approach recognizes the potential asymmetry between developed and developing countries in the market for technology transfer, and so includes provisions that seek to encourage cooperation and assistance for developing countries in evolving their own technological base and R&D facilities, and the granting of incentives to TNCs by their home countries so as to encourage technology transfer to developing countries. Thus, it abandons the willingness to prohibit specific terms in technology transfer transactions that is characteristic of the "regulatory" approach, relying rather on competition rules to control abuses. The "regulatory" approach is characteristic of instruments concluded by developing countries in the 1960s and 1970s, of which the Andean Community's Decision 24 is the leading example. It can also be discerned in the provisions of the draft TOT Code. The "market-based development" approach is characteristic of more recent agreements and finds its fullest expression in the TRIPS Agreement (Roffe, 2000).

A variant of the second approach may be seen to be emerging in relation to environmental issues. As noted in Section I, provisions for the transfer of environmentally sound technology to developing countries are increasingly common in international environmental agreements. For example, the United Nations Framework Convention on Climate Change and its Kyoto Protocol contain specific provisions with regard to the transfer and development of technology. These instruments have as their starting point the free commercial transfer of technology by TNCs, but subject to the need to ensure that such transfers are not harmful in environmental terms and that TNCs are encouraged to transfer environmentally sound technologies to developing countries which may otherwise have no opportunity to use them. For example, Article 19 of the Energy Charter Treaty encourages the sharing of technical information on environmentally sound technologies and the transfer of such technologies subject to the adequate and effective protection of IPRs. Equally, the Biodiversity Convention establishes a link between "appropriate" access to and utilization of genetic resources, on the one hand, and "appropriate" transfer of relevant technology to developing countries (including those subject to patents and other intellectual property rights), on the other hand. This link is expressly acknowledged as part of the objectives of the Convention, which are:

> "the conservation of biological diversity, the sustainable use of its components and the fair and equitable sharing of the benefits arising out of the utilization of genetic resources, including by appropriate access to genetic resources, and by appropriate transfer of relevant technologies, taking into account all rights over those resources and to technologies, and by appropriate funding" (ILM, 1992, p. 64).

As these provisions are fully covered in this Series by the paper on *Environment* (UNCTAD, 2001b), no further mention will be made of them here. (For ease of reference, annex table 1 contains a list of selected instruments in the area of environment and their technology-transfer provisions.)

The third approach, which may be termed the "intra-regional technology development" approach, has been adopted in regional economic development agreements between developing countries. These agreements differ from the "regulatory" model in that they concentrate on the encouragement of intra-regional technology development and transfer whether through regional industrial policies or through the establishment of specialized regimes for regional multinational enterprises. They do not deal as such with technology transfer by investors from outside the region. Nor can these agreements be seen as examples of the "market-based development" approach in that they are firmly committed to the development of member country sponsored industrial development policies. However, they may be closer in spirit to this approach as these regional agreements do not subject the inward transfer of technology by investors from outside the region to strict regulatory controls.

1. The "regulatory" approach

This approach was followed in the national laws and policies of numerous countries during the 1970s, following a model well established in Japan and the Republic of Korea (Omer, 2001, pp. 301-303). It is most fully exemplified on the regional level by the Andean Community's policy on technology imports, as contained in Decision 24 of 31 December 1970, the "Common Regulations Governing Foreign Capital Movement, Trade Marks, Patents, Licences and Royalties", which has since been superseded (UNCTAD, 1996a, vol. II, p. 454). The aims of Decision 24 included the strengthening of national undertakings in the Andean Community so as to equip them to participate actively in the subregional market. One means by which this was to be achieved was to ensure that national undertakings had "the fullest possible access to modern technology and contemporary managerial innovations" (UNCTAD, 1996a, vol. II, p. 455). This, in turn, was to be achieved by way of a system of screening of technology transfer agreements by the authorities of the member countries. Thus, under Article 18 of Decision 24:

> "Every agreement relating to the import of technology or to patents and trade marks shall be examined and submitted for approval to the competent authority of the member country, which shall assess the effective contribution of the imported technology by estimating the benefits likely to be obtained from it, the price of the goods in which it is embodied, and any other quantifiable effect it may have" (UNCTAD, 1996a, vol. II, p. 460).

Such national regulation was to be subject to certain guiding principles contained in Decision 24. Thus, Article 19 prescribed that certain minimum provisions had to be included in a technology transfer agreement regarding the particular form of transfer, the contractual value of the transfer and the duration of the agreement. Article 20 prohibited the authorization of the conclusion of technology transfer agreements where these contained certain conditions. These included undertakings in relation to the purchase of capital goods, intermediate products, raw materials or other forms of technology, or in relation to the employment of staff designated by the transfer or undertaking; resale price maintenance provisions; production restrictions; no competing technology use clauses; technology purchase options and grant backs favourable to the transferor; and royalty payments on unused patents and other conditions of equivalent effect. Also, export restrictions on products containing the transferred technology were not permitted. Article 21 ensured that royalty payments could not be treated as transfers of capital, and that such transfers between affiliates in a TNC would be subject to tax.

Alongside this screening procedure, Decision 24 established a programme for the encouragement of regional technological development and for the adaptation and assimilation of existing technologies. To this end, the member countries would be obliged to monitor technological developments in particular industries so as to identify the most useful technologies and processes, and a system of incentives for the production of technology, export promotion schemes for products incorporating regional technology, and preferential purchasing programmes for such products within the region were to be established (Decision 24, Articles 22-24, in UNCTAD, 1996a, vol. II, p. 461). Finally, under Article 25 certain restrictive conditions in trademark licensing agreements were prohibited, and under Article 26 the Andean Commission was enabled to declare that certain production processes or groups of products would not be able to enjoy patent privileges in any member country. This covered both future and existing privileges.

Decision 24 was superseded by Decision 220, which was in turn superseded by Decision 291 of 21 March 1991, which now represents Andean Community policy in this area (UNCTAD, 1996a, vol. II, p. 447). While this latter Decision mainly concerns the reform of the Andean Community member States' policies on inward FDI, it retained, in Chapter IV, certain provisions on technology imports that display some features of the regulatory approach taken in Decision 24. The major difference is that the Andean Commission leaves more freedom to member countries to formulate their national laws in this field. Thus, under Article 12 of Decision 291, member countries shall register, with the relevant national agency, contracts for technology licensing, technical assistance, technical services, basic and special engineering and other technological contracts, as defined in the applicable national laws. That agency shall then evaluate the effective contribution of the imported technology by estimating its probable uses and the cost of goods incorporating the technology, or by otherwise measuring the specific impact of the technology. Decision 291 retains similar provisions to those found in Decision 24 concerning the minimum clauses to be contained in a technology transfer agreement, although it adds a requirement to identify the parties, with specific mention of their nationality and domicile. Article 14 then reproduces the same list of "blacklisted" clauses that should not be included in technology transfer agreements as those found in Article 20 of Decision 24. However, this is done with the important difference that, in place of the absolute prohibition found in Article 20 of Decision 24, Article 14 of Decision 291 requires only that member countries "shall ensure" that technology importation contracts do not contain these clauses. In addition, Article 15 of Decision 291 liberalizes the prohibition on the treatment of royalties on transferred technology as capital investment, and allows this subject to the payment of tax on the royalties. Finally the programme on regional technological development, established by Decision 24, is no longer mentioned in Decision 291.

The regulatory approach to the encouragement of technology transfer to developing countries was a significant feature of initiatives on the regulation of TNCs undertaken by various United Nations bodies in the 1970s and 1980s.[4] Thus United Nations General Assembly

Resolution 3202 (S-VI), the Declaration on the Establishment of a New International Economic Order, requires respect for the principle of "giving to the developing countries access to the achievements of modern science and technology, and promoting the transfer of technology and the creation of indigenous technology for the benefit of the developing countries in forms and in accordance with procedures which are suited to their economies" (UNCTAD, 1996a, vol. I, p. 50). This principle is given some form by United Nations General Assembly Resolution 3202 (S-VI), the Programme of Action on the Establishment of a New International Economic Order, which asserts that all efforts should be made to formulate an international code of conduct for the transfer of technology corresponding to the needs and conditions prevalent in developing countries, to give improved access on the part of developing countries to modern technology; to adapt that technology to their needs; to expand significantly the assistance from developed to developing countries in R&D programmes and in the creation of suitable indigenous technology; to adapt commercial practices governing technology transfer to the requirements of developing countries and to prevent the abuse of rights of sellers; and to promote international cooperation and R&D in exploration and exploitation, conservation and the legitimate utilization of natural resources and all sources of energy. In addition, the Programme of Action envisages, as part of the agenda for the regulation of and control over the activities of TNCs, an international code of conduct for TNCs which would aim *inter alia* "to bring about assistance, transfer of technology and management skills to developing countries on equitable and favourable terms" (UNCTAD, 1996a, vol. I, pp. 53-54). In a similar vein, United Nations General Assembly Resolution 3281 (XXIX), the Charter on the Economic Rights and Duties of States, provides in Article 13(4) that "All States should co-operate in research with a view to evolving further internationally accepted guidelines or regulations for the transfer of technology, taking fully into account the interests of the developing countries" (UNCTAD, 1996a, vol. I, p. 64).

check if this was passed.

Following on from these policy-making United Nations resolutions, the draft United Nations Code of Conduct on Transnational Corporations contained a general provision on technology transfer that exemplifies the "regulatory" approach to this issue. Under paragraph 36 of the Code, TNCs have the following duties:

"•   To conform to the technology transfer laws and regulations of the countries in which they operate.

•   To co-operate with the authorities of those countries in assessing the impact of international transfers of technology in their economies and consult with them regarding various technological options which might help those countries, particularly developing countries, to attain their economic and social development.

•   In their transfer of technology transactions, including intra-corporate transactions, to avoid practices which adversely affect the international flow of technology, or otherwise hinder the economic and technological development of countries, particularly developing countries.

•   To contribute to the strengthening of the scientific and technological capacities of developing countries, in accordance with the science and technology policies and priorities of those countries and to undertake substantial R&D activities in developing countries and make full use of local resources and personnel in this process" (UNCTAD, 1996a, vol. I, pp. 168-169).

The draft Code of Conduct ends by referring to the applicability of the relevant provisions of the draft TOT Code for the purposes of the draft Code of Conduct, thereby emphazising the supremacy of the specialized code in relation to issues concerning technology transfer.

The draft TOT Code, which was negotiated under the auspices of UNCTAD between 1976 and 1985, represents the high benchmark for a model of provisions espousing the "regulatory" approach to technology transfer (UNCTAD, 1996a, vol. I, p.181; see also Patel et al., 2001). This is exemplified, in particular, by the objectives and principles of the draft TOT Code in Chapter 2 and by the provisions on the national regulation of technology transfer transactions in Chapter 3. These are reproduced in full in box.II.4. In particular, emphasis is placed, in the objectives section of Chapter 2, on the encouragement of technology transfer transactions involving developing countries, under conditions in which the bargaining positions of the parties are balanced so as to avoid abuses of a stronger position and thereby to achieve mutually satisfactory agreements. Furthermore, the "unpackaging" of technology is recommended, as are the specification of restrictive business practices from which parties to technology transfer transactions ought to, or be obliged to, refrain and the laying down of an appropriate set of responsibilities and obligations of parties to transfer of technology transactions, taking into account not only their legitimate interests but also differences in their bargaining positions. All of these objectives are consistent with a "regulatory" approach to technology transfer.

Box II.4. Draft International Code of Conduct on the Transfer of Technology (1985 version)

"Chapter 2
Objectives and Principles

2. The Code of Conduct is based on the following objectives and principles:

2.1. Objectives

(i) To establish general and equitable standards on which to base the relationship among parties to transfer of technology transactions and

/...

Box II.4 (continued)

governments concerned, taking into consideration their legitimate interests, and giving due recognition to special needs of developing countries for the fulfilment of their economic and social development objectives.

(ii) To promote mutual confidence between parties as well as their governments.

(iii) To encourage transfer of technology transactions, particularly those involving developing countries, under conditions where bargaining positions of the parties to the transactions are balanced in such a way as to avoid abuses of a stronger position and thereby to achieve mutually satisfactory agreements.

(iv) To facilitate and increase the international flow of technological information, particularly on the availability of alternative technologies, as a prerequisite for the assessment, selection, adaptation, development and use of technologies in all countries, particularly developing countries.

(v) To facilitate and increase the international flow of proprietary and non-proprietary technology for strengthening growth of the scientific and technological capabilities of all countries, particularly developing countries, so as to increase their participation in world production and trade.

(vi) To increase the contributions of technology to the identification and solution of social and economic problems of all countries, particularly the developing countries, including the development of basic sectors of their national economies.

(vii) To facilitate the formulation, adoption and implementation of national policies, laws and regulations on the subject of transfer of technology by setting forth international norms.

(viii) To promote adequate arrangements as regards unpackaging in terms of information concerning the various elements of the technology to be transferred, such as that required for technical, institutional and financial evaluation of the transaction, thus avoiding undue or unnecessary packaging.

(ix) To specify restrictive [business] practices from which parties to technology transfer transactions [shall] [should] refrain. *

/...

Box II.4 (continued)

(x) To set forth an appropriate set of responsibilities and obligations of parties to transfer of technology transactions, taking into consideration their legitimate interests as well as differences in their bargaining positions.

2.2. Principles

(i)   The Code of Conduct is universally applicable in scope.

(ii)   States have the right to adopt all appropriate measures for facilitating and regulating the transfer of technology, in a manner consistent with their international obligations, taking into consideration the legitimate interests of all parties concerned, and encouraging transfer of technology under mutually agreed, fair and reasonable terms and conditions.

(iii) The principles of sovereignty and political independence of States (covering, inter alia, the requirements of foreign policy and national security) and sovereign equality of States, should be recognized in facilitating and regulating transfer of technology transactions.

(iv) States should co-operate in the international transfer of technology in order to promote economic growth throughout the world, especially that of the developing countries. Co-operation in such transfer should be irrespective of any differences in political, economic and social systems; this is one of the important elements in maintaining international peace and security and promoting international economic stability and progress, the general welfare of nations and international co-operation free from discrimination based on such differences. Nothing in this Code may be construed as impairing or derogating from the provisions of the Charter of the United Nations or actions taken in pursuance thereof. It is understood that special treatment in transfer of technology should be accorded to developing countries in accordance with the provisions in this Code on the subject.

(v) The separate responsibilities of parties to transfer of technology transactions, on the one hand, and those of governments when not acting as parties, on the other, should be clearly distinguished.

(vi) Mutual benefits should accrue to technology supplying and recipient parties in order to maintain and increase the international flow of technology.

/...

Box II.4 (continued)

(vii) Facilitating and increasing the access to technology, particularly for developing countries, under mutually agreed fair and reasonable terms and conditions, are fundamental elements in the process of technology transfer and development.

(viii) Recognition of the protection of industrial property rights granted under national law.

(ix) Technology supplying parties when operating in an acquiring country should respect the sovereignty and the laws of that country, act with proper regard for that country's declared development policies and priorities and endeavour to contribute substantially to the development of the acquiring country. The freedom of parties to negotiate, conclude and perform agreements for the transfer of technology on mutually acceptable terms and conditions should be based on respect for the foregoing and other principles set forth in this Code.

Chapter 3
National regulation of transfer of technology transactions

3.1 In adopting, and in the light of evolving circumstances making necessary changes in laws, regulations and rules, and policies with respect to transfer of technology transactions, States have the right to adopt measures such as those listed in paragraph 3.4 of this chapter and should act on the basis that these measures should:

(i) Recognize that a close relationship exists between technology flows [and] the conditions under which such flows are admitted and treated;

(ii) Promote a favourable and beneficial climate for the international transfer of technology;

(iii) Take into consideration in an equitable manner the legitimate interests of all parties;

(iv) Encourage and facilitate transfers of technology to take place under mutually agreed, fair and reasonable terms and conditions having regard to the principles and objectives of the Code;

(v) Take into account the differing factors characterizing the transactions such as local conditions, the nature of the technology and the scope of the undertaking;

/...

Box II.4 (continued)

(vi) Be consistent with their international obligations.

3.2. Measures adopted by States including decisions of competent administrative bodies should be applied fairly, equitably, and on the same basis to all parties in accordance with established procedures of law and the principles and objectives of the Code. Laws and regulations should be clearly defined and publicly and readily available. To the extent appropriate, relevant information regarding decisions of competent administrative bodies should be disseminated.

3.3. Each country adopting legislation on the protection of industrial property should have regard to its national needs of economic and social development, and should ensure an effective protection of industrial property rights granted under its national law and other related rights recognized by its national law.

3.4. Measures on regulation of the flows and effects of transfer of technology, finance and technical aspects of technology transactions and on organizational forms and mechanisms may deal with:

Finance
(a) Currency regulations of foreign exchange payments and remittances;
(b) Conditions of domestic credit and financing facilities;
(c) Transferability of payments;
(d) Tax treatment;
(e) Pricing policies;

Renegotiation
(f) Terms, conditions and objective criteria for the renegotiation of transfer of technology transactions;

Technical aspects
(g) Technology specifications and standards for the various components of the transfer of technology transactions and their payments;
(h) Analysis and evaluation of transfer of technology transactions to assist parties in their negotiation;
(i) Use of local and imported components;

/...

As for the principles underlying the draft TOT Code, these too include provisions that further a regulatory agenda. Thus, *inter alia,* States are said to have the right to adopt all appropriate measures for facilitating and regulating the transfer of technology and to enjoy recognition of the principles of sovereignty and political independence and sovereign equality of States in this process. Furthermore, among the fundamental elements in the process of technology transfer and development, the draft TOT Code includes facilitating and increasing access to technology, particularly for developing countries, under mutually agreed fair and reasonable terms and conditions and the recognition of the protection of IPRs granted under national law.

Box II.4 (continued)

Organizational forms and mechanisms

(j) Evaluation, negotiation, and registration of transfer of technology transactions;

(k) Terms, conditions, duration, of transfer of technology transactions;

(l) Loss of ownership and/or control of domestic acquiring enterprises;

(m) Regulation of foreign collaboration arrangements and agreements that could displace national enterprises from the domestic market;

(n) The definition of fields of activity of foreign enterprises and the choice of channels, mechanisms, organizational forms for the transfer of technology and the prior or subsequent approval of transfer of technology transactions and their registration in these fields;

(o) The determination of the legal effect of transactions which are not in conformity with national laws, regulations and administrative decisions on the transfer of technology;

(p) The establishment or strengthening of national administrative mechanisms for the implementation and application of the Code of Conduct and of national laws, regulations and policies on the transfer of technology;

(q) Promotion of appropriate channels for the international exchange of information and experience in the field of the transfer of technology."

Source: UNCTAD, 1996a, vol. I, pp.184-188.

Note: * Text under consideration.

Chapter 3 of the draft TOT Code (box II.4) also stresses the right of States to regulate technology transfers in any of the ways listed in paragraph 3.4. thereof, subject to a non-binding obligation[5] to take into account the six requirements listed in paragraph 3.1.

The regulatory approach of the draft TOT Code continues in its treatment of restrictive business practices in Chapter 4 (to be discussed in the next subsection), and through the laying down of detailed provisions concerning the responsibilities and obligations of the parties to a technology transfer agreement in Chapter 5. These start with an exhortation to the parties to be responsive to the economic and social objectives of the respective countries, and particularly those of the technology-acquiring country, when negotiating and concluding such an agreement. Furthermore, the parties should observe fair and honest business practices in their dealings. Chapter 5 goes on to enumerate various specific matters that should be considered by the parties at the negotiating phase, including the use of locally available resources, rendering of technical services and unpackaging. As to fair and honest business negotiating practices, Chapter 5 of the draft TOT Code recommends that both parties should negotiate fair and reasonable terms and conditions in good faith, offer relevant information to each other, keep secret confidential information received from the other party and cease negotiations if no satisfactory agreement can be reached. Chapter 5 then continues with provisions concerning the need to disclose relevant information about the development needs and regulatory environment of the recipient's country and about the nature of the technology concerned. Chapter 5 concludes with a list of mutually acceptable contractual obligations that should be included in the agreement. These relate to access to improvements, confidentiality, dispute settlement and applicable law, description of the technology, suitability for use, rights to the technology transferred, quality levels and goodwill, performance guarantees, transmission of relevant technical documentation, training of personnel and provision of accessories, spare parts and components, and liability (UNCTAD, 1996a, vol. I, pp. 194-195).

The draft TOT Code ends with three chapters dedicated to improving the access of countries, particularly developing countries, to technology. Thus, Chapter 6 offers provisions for the special treatment of developing countries by developed countries; Chapter 7 provides for international collaboration with a view to facilitating an expanded international flow of technology aimed at strengthening the technological capabilities of all countries; and Chapter 8 envisages an international institutional machinery for the development of the TOT Code to be placed under the auspices of UNCTAD. Of these, Chapter 6 in particular needs closer examination (box II.5).

Box II.5. Draft International Code of Conduct on the Transfer of Technology
(1985 version)

"Chapter 6
Special treatment for developing countries

6.1. Taking into consideration the needs and problems of developing countries, particularly of the least developed countries, governments of developed countries, directly or through appropriate international organizations, in order to facilitate and encourage the initiation and strengthening of the scientific and technological capabilities of developing countries so as to assist and co-operate with them in their efforts to fulfil their economic and social objectives, should take adequate specific measures, *inter alia*, to:
(i) facilitate access by developing countries to available information regarding the availabilities, description, location and, as far as possible, approximate cost of technologies which might help those countries to attain their economic and social development objectives;
(ii) give developing countries the freest and fullest possible access to technologies whose transfer is not subject to private decisions; *

/...

Box II.5 (continued)

(iii) facilitate access by developing countries, to the extent practicable, to technologies whose transfer is subject to private decisions; *

(iv) assist and co-operate with developing countries in the assessment and adaptation of existing technologies and in the development of national technologies by facilitating access, as far as possible, to available scientific and industrial research data;

(v) co-operate in the development of scientific and technological resources in developing countries, including the creation and growth of innovative capacities;

(vi) assist developing countries in strengthening their technological capacity, especially in the basic sectors of their national economy, through creation of and support for laboratories, experimental facilities and institutes for training and research;

(vii) co-operate in the establishment or strengthening of national, regional and/or international institutions, including transfer centres, to help developing countries to develop and obtain technology and skills required for the establishment, development and enhancement of their technological capabilities including the design, construction and operation of plants;

(viii) encourage the adaptation of research and development, engineering and design to conditions and factor endowments prevailing in developing countries;

(ix) co-operate in measures leading to greater utilization of the managerial, engineering, design and technical experience of the personnel and the institutions of developing countries in specific economic and other development projects undertaken at the bilateral and multilateral levels;

(x) encourage the training of personnel from developing countries.

6.2. Governments of developed countries, directly or through appropriate international organizations, in assisting in the promotion of transfer of technology to developing countries - particularly to the least developed countries - should, as a part of programmes for development assistance and co-operation, take into account requests from developing countries to:

/...

Box II.5 (continued)

(i)   contribute to the development of national technologies in developing countries by providing experts under development assistance and research exchange programmes;

(ii)   provide training for research, engineering, design and other personnel from developing countries engaged in the development of national technologies or in the adaptation and use of technologies transferred;

(iii) provide assistance and co-operation in the development and administration of laws and regulations with a view to facilitating the transfer of technology;

(iv) provide support for projects in developing countries for the development and adaptation of new and existing technologies suitable to the particular needs of developing countries;

(v)   grant credits on terms more favourable than the usual commercial terms for financing the acquisition of capital and intermediate goods in the context of approved development projects involving transfer of technology transactions so as to reduce the cost of projects and improve the quality of technology received by the developing countries;

(vi) provide assistance and co-operation in the development and administration of laws and regulations designed to avoid health, safety and environmental risks associated with technology or the products produced by it.

6.3. Governments of developed countries should take measures in accordance with national policies, laws and regulations to encourage and to endeavour to give incentives to enterprises and institutions in their countries, either individually or in collaboration with enterprises and institutions in developing countries, particularly those in the least developed countries, to make special efforts, *inter alia*, to:

(i)   assist in the development of technological capabilities of the enterprises in developing countries, including special training as required by the recipients;

(ii)   undertake the development of technology appropriate to the needs of developing countries;

/...

In essence, Chapter 6 urges the Governments of developed countries, directly or through international organizations, to facilitate and encourage the initiation and strengthening of the technological capabilities of developing countries through the types of measures listed in box II.5. Thus an expectation of information exchange and cooperation in the technology transfer field is envisaged. This entails taking into account requests from developing countries concerning *inter alia* the establishment of research assistance programmes, the development of new laws and regulations, work on specific projects and access to favourable finance and credit. Furthermore, developed countries should encourage their enterprises to become involved in such activities through government-led programmes.

Box II.5 (concluded)

(iii) undertake R and D activity in developing countries of interest to such countries, as well as to improve co-operation between enterprises and scientific and technological institutions of developed and developing countries;

(iv) assist in projects by enterprises and institutions in developing countries for the development and adaptation of new and existing technologies suitable to the particular needs and conditions of developing countries.

6.4. The special treatment accorded to developing countries should be responsive to their economic and social objectives vis-a-vis their relative stage of economic and social development and with particular attention to the special problems and conditions of the least developed countries."

Source: UNCTAD, 1996a, vol. I, pp. 195-197.

Note: * The term "private decision" in the particular context of this chapter should be officially interpreted in the light of the legal order of the respective country.

---

2. The market-based development approach

This approach is best exemplified by the technology transfer related provisions of the TRIPS Agreement. As noted in the previous section, Articles 7 and 8 of the TRIPS Agreement provide that the protection of IPRs should contribute to the promotion of technological innovation, and the transfer and dissemination of technology, to the mutual advantage of producers and users of technological knowledge and in a manner conducive to social and economic welfare, and to a balance of rights and obligations. This policy is further developed in Article 66 (2) of the TRIPS Agreement whereby "[d]eveloped country Members shall provide incentives to enterprises and institutions in their territories for the purpose of promoting and encouraging technology transfer to least developed country Members in order to enable them to create a sound and viable technological base". This is to be reinforced through an obligation, under Article 67, for developed country members to provide, on request and on mutually agreed terms and conditions, technical and financial cooperation in favour of developing and least developed country members in order to facilitate the implementation of the TRIPS Agreement.

However, notwithstanding these specific provisions on technology transfer, the main thrust of the TRIPS Agreement is the protection of IPRs based on the principles described in Section A above and on competition related provisions to be described in Section C below. The underlying policy is centred on the belief that the encouragement of technology transfer is best achieved in an environment in which IPRs are fully protected as private commercial property and in which the market for technology is maintained in as competitive a condition as possible. Thus the emphasis has shifted away from the regulation of technology transfer transactions in the interests of the weaker party - normally the recipient in the developing country - towards a more open market-based model in which increased technology transfer to developing countries is to be encouraged through the proper operation of the market, coupled with assistance and cooperation on the part of developed countries. Thus this is not an approach that completely abandons governmental action on policy. Rather, there is a move away from the regulatory control of transactions by recipient developing country Governments towards the encouragement of increased levels of technology transfer through governmental programmes, and incentives to firms, on the part of developed country Governments.

A similar approach can be found in the Energy Charter Treaty, the General Agreement on Trade in Services (GATS) and the recently revised OECD Guidelines for Multinational Enterprises. Thus Article 8 of the Energy Charter Treaty calls upon signatories "to promote access to and transfer of technology in the field of energy technology on a commercial and non-discriminatory basis to assist effective trade in Energy Materials and Products and Investment and to implement the objectives of the Charter subject to their laws and regulations, and to the protection of intellectual property rights". This provision continues by requiring the signatories to eliminate existing obstacles to the transfer of technology in this field and to create no new ones (UNCTAD, 1996a, vol. II, pp. 553-554).

In the field of services, Article IV (1) (a) of the GATS Agreement recognizes that, in order to increase the participation of developing countries in world trade, further negotiations should be pursued to strengthen their domestic services capacity, their efficiency and competitiveness, "*inter alia* through access to technology on a commercial basis". Furthermore, developed country members should establish contact points with developing and least developed country members to supply information concerning, among other things, the availability of services technology (GATS Article IV (2)(c), in UNCTAD, 1996a, vol. I, p. 290). In relation to the objectives set out in Article IV of the GATS, Article XIX makes clear that developing country members are able to make the liberalization of market access to foreign service providers subject to conditions that aim to achieve those objectives. Thus a degree of developing host country regulation over entry conditions is accepted where this is likely to enhance a given country's access to technology. Finally, the GATS Annex on Telecommunications commits developed country members, where practical, to making available to developing countries information on telecommunications services and developments in telecommunications technology to assist in strengthening their domestic telecommunications services sector.

Other WTO instruments may also be mentioned briefly, in that their terms seek to contribute to the promotion of technology transfer from developed to developing countries. Thus the Agreement on Subsidies and Countervailing Measures includes, within its definition of non-actionable subsidies in Article 8, matters of import to technology transfer such as research activities, assistance to disadvantaged regions and the adaptation of existing facilities to new environmental requirements. Similarly, the Agreement on Technical Barriers to Trade recognizes, in its preamble, the positive contribution that international standardization of technical requirements can make to the transfer of technology from developed to developing countries. Article 11 of the Agreement goes on to encourage developed country members to give technical assistance to developing country members in the field of standardization, while Article 12.4 specifically accepts that developing countries may adopt technical standards aimed at the preservation of indigenous technology and production methods and processes compatible with their development needs.

The OECD Guidelines for Multinational Enterprises also follow a market-based development approach. Thus chapter VIII of the Guidelines encourages enterprises to adopt, where practicable, practices that permit the transfer and rapid diffusion of technologies and know-how, with due regard to the protection of IPRs (OECD, 2000, p. 26). Although the Guidelines do not specifically mention developing countries, given that enterprises are expected to "[c]ontribute to economic, social and environmental progress with a view to achieving sustainable development" (ibid., p. 19; chapter II, General Policies, paragraph 1), the Guideline on Science and Technology can be read with the special needs of developing host countries in mind. This is reinforced by the OECD's Commentary on the Science and Technology Guideline, which states that access to technology generated by TNCs is "important for the realization of economy wide effects of technological progress, including productivity growth and job creation, within the context of sustainable development" (ibid., p. 52). Accordingly, when the Guidelines refer to the need for enterprises to "perform science and technology development work in host countries to address local market needs, as well as employ host country personnel in a [science and technology] capacity and encourage their training, taking into account commercial needs" they can be understood as introducing development-oriented considerations that ought to be taken into account by enterprises when determining their science and technology policy. This is reinforced by paragraph 1 of chapter VIII, which states that enterprises should:

> "Endeavour to ensure that their activities are compatible with the science and technology (S &T) policies and plans of the countries in which they operate and as appropriate contribute to the development of local and national innovative capacity" (OECD, 2000, p. 26).

It is arguable that, insofar as TNC involvement in host country science and technology policy is concerned, the text of the Guidelines suggests that an element of regulation is desirable as a supplement to market-based policies. Equally, although the Guidelines do not differentiate between developed and developing host countries – and so do not require more favourable treatment of the latter – should TNCs observe the above provisions in their science and technology operations in developing countries, this may go some way to meeting the special needs of such countries. However, it should not be forgotten that the Guidelines are voluntary instruments and so no binding obligations are imposed on TNCs. It is within the discretion of TNCs to decide how they will discharge their obligations in this regard. On the other hand, there is nothing in the Guidelines to rule out binding commitments in this area being required of TNCs as a matter of national law, provided that these do not violate other international agreements to which a country is party. Thus the OECD Guidelines, though supporting a discretionary approach on the part of TNCs in relation to their science and technology obligations, do not appear to regard a degree of regulation in this regard as being incompatible with a predominantly market-based approach to technology transfer issues.

The adoption of a market-based approach to technology transfer issues can also be discerned in the various cooperation agreements concluded by the EU with developing countries. The Fourth Lomé Convention of 1989 contained numerous commitments on the part of the EU to assist in the transfer and acquisition of technology by the developing States parties to the Convention in a variety of fields, including agricultural and industrial cooperation, energy and tourism (UNCTAD, 1996a, vol. II, p. 385). The more recent Cotonou Agreement of 2000 revises this approach, further emphasizing the market-led policy on technology transfer. Accordingly, under Article 23 (j) cooperation between the EU and developing contracting parties in the field of economic sector development includes the development of scientific, technological and research infrastructure and services, including the enhancement, transfer and absorption of new technologies. This is to be achieved in the context of the general policy behind the Cotonou Agreement to encourage developing country parties to integrate more fully into the global economy. Of particular relevance also is the commitment of all parties, in Article 46, to ensuring an adequate and effective level of protection of IPRs and other rights covered by the TRIPS Agreement. This includes an agreement to strengthen cooperation on the preparation and enforcement of laws and regulations in this field, the setting up of administrative offices and the training of personnel (EC, 2000). In a similar vein, agreements concluded between the EU and Latin American economic integration groups contain a commitment to economic cooperation that includes the encouragement of technology transfer.[6]

Finally, although almost all BITs are silent on the question of technology transfer, it should be noted that the Dutch model agreement of 1997 states, in its preamble, that "agreement upon the treatment to be accorded to investments [by the nationals of one Contracting Party in the territory of the other Contracting Party] will stimulate the flow of capital and technology and the economic development of the Contracting Parties" (UNCTAD, 2000b, vol. V, p. 333). Thus the Dutch model agreement makes a clear connection between the promotion and protection of investors and their investments and the stimulation of technology transfer. In that sense, it could be said that such a policy may be seen as part of the market-based development approach, as it aims for the creation of market conditions conducive to increased investment which, in turn, may lead to increased transfers of technology as part of the investment process.

3. The intra-regional technology development approach

As noted above, certain intra-regional economic integration agreements contain provisions encouraging the development and transfer of technology by enterprises operating within the region. These may be divided into two main groups: general provisions stressing cooperation in areas relevant to the development and transfer of technology within the region, and specialized provisions establishing regional multinational enterprises, which in turn have an obligation to develop technology and transfer it across the region.

As to the first group, certain recent agreements concluded by African States display provisions that encourage, in general terms, the development of industrial policies that may facilitate the evolution of intra-regional technology. Thus the Treaty Establishing the African Economic Community of 1991 calls upon the Community to harmonize national policies on science and technology and to promote technical cooperation and the exchange of experience in the field of industrial technology and implement technical training programmes among member States (Articles 4(2)(e) and 49(h), in UNCTAD, 2000b, vol. V, pp. 16-18). A similar commitment can be found in Article 26 (3)(i) of the Revised Treaty of the Economic Community of West African States (ECOWAS) of 1993 (UNCTAD, 2000b, vol. V, p. 40), and in Articles 100 (d) and 103 (2) of the Treaty Establishing the Common Market for Eastern and Southern Africa (COMESA) of 1993 (UNCTAD, 1996a, vol. III, p. 102).

As to the second group of provisions, a good example comes from the COMESA Treaty. Under Article 101 (2) (iv), the multinational industrial enterprises that are to be set up under the Treaty are expected to enhance the "development or acquisition of modern technology, managerial and marketing experience" (UNCTAD, 1996a, vol. III, p. 103). Equally the Multinational Companies Code in the Customs and Economic Union of Central Africa (UDEAC) of 1975 states that multinational companies are set up under this agreement *inter alia* for the purpose of "encouraging and facilitating the transfer of technology by associating national counterparts with the activities and studies of foreign experts" (Chapter 1.1(g), in UNCTAD, 1996a, vol. II, p. 175). The above-mentioned African Economic Community Treaty also envisages, in Article 48(2)(b), the creation of African multinational enterprises in priority industries, as does Article 26(2)(b) of the Revised ECOWAS Treaty. Finally, the Agreement for the Establishment of a Regime for CARICOM Enterprises should be mentioned in that, according to its preamble, this regime was established in part to further the development of a regional technological capacity in the production of goods and services on a regional basis for both the regional and extra-regional markets (UNCTAD, 1996a, vol. II, p. 267). More recently, the Protocol amending the CARICOM Treaty in the Field of Industrial

Policy re-emphasized, in the preamble, the "imperatives of research and development and technology transfer and adaptation for the competitiveness of Community enterprises on a sustainable basis". It would appear that this organization is now moving towards a general regime of market-led industrial development, in which specific policies for technology transfer are giving way to general policies on market-led, internationally competitive and sustainable production of goods and services (UNCTAD, 2000b, vol. IV, pp. 219-226).

C. Competition-related provisions

The control of restrictive business practices (RBPs) in technology transfer agreements has contributed to the development of important provisions on this matter in international instruments. Indeed, as noted in Section I, it was disagreement over the nature and extent of such control that was at the heart of the non-adoption of the draft TOT Code. At least two major approaches to this question can be identified. The first, which belongs to the "regulatory" model of encouraging technology transfer mentioned in the previous subsection, requires that RBPs that interfere with the full, open and effective transfer of technology should be prohibited, even though there may be good economic reasons for permitting a degree of restriction on the freedom of the technology recipient to use the transferred technology as they wish. The second approach, which follows as part of the "market-based development" model discussed above, bases the control of RBPs in this area upon a test of whether the restriction in question is reasonable, taking account of the interests of both the transferor and the recipient.

The first approach is exemplified in the draft TOT Code. It contained a more specific treatment of RBPs in relation to technology transfer in its Chapter 4 (box II.6). This part of the draft Code was to prove one of the hardest to negotiate and, indeed, the failure to agree on its terms was a major reason for the eventual non-adoption of the

Box II.6. Draft International Code of Conduct on the Transfer of Technology (1985 version)

"Chapter 4 a/

[The regulation of practices and arrangements involving the transfer of technology] [Restrictive business practices]
[Exclusion of political discrimination and restrictive business practices] b/

Section A: (Chapeau) c/

Section B: (List of practices) d/

1. [Exclusive] ** Grant-back provisions e/

Requiring the acquiring party to transfer or grant back to the supplying party, or to any other enterprise designated by the supplying party, improvements arising from the acquired technology, on an exclusive basis [or]* without offsetting consideration or reciprocal obligations from the supplying party, or when the practice will constitute an abuse of a dominant market position of the supplying party.

2. Challenges to validity e/

[Unreasonably] ** requiring the acquiring party to refrain from challenging the validity of patents and other types of protection for inventions involved in the transfer or the validity of other such grants claimed or obtained by the supplying party, recognizing that any issues concerning the mutual rights and obligations of the parties following such a challenge will be determined by the appropriate applicable law and the terms of the agreement to the extent consistent with that law. f/

3. Exclusive dealing

Restrictions on the freedom of the acquiring party to enter into sales, representation or manufacturing agreements relating to similar or competing technologies or products or to obtain competing technology, when such restrictions are not needed for ensuring the achievement of
/...

Box II.6 (continued)

legitimate interests, particularly including securing the confidentiality of the technology transferred or best effort distribution or promotional obligations.

4. Restrictions on research e/

[Unreasonably]**/*** restricting the acquiring party either in undertaking research and development directed to absorb and adapt the transferred technology to local conditions or in initiating research and development programmes in connection with new products, processes or equipment.

5. Restrictions on use of personnel e/

[Unreasonably] ** requiring the acquiring party to use personnel designated by the supplying party, except to the extent necessary to ensure the efficient transmission phase for the transfer of technology and putting it to use or thereafter continuing such requirement beyond the time when adequately trained local personnel are available or have been trained; or prejudicing the use of personnel of the technology acquiring country.

6. Price fixing e/

[Unjustifiably]** imposing regulation of prices to be charged by acquiring parties in the relevant market to which the technology was transferred for products manufactured or services produced using the technology supplied.

7. Restrictions on adaptations e/

Restrictions which [unreasonably]** prevent the acquiring party from adapting the imported technology to local conditions or introducing innovations in it, or which oblige the acquiring party to introduce unwanted or unnecessary design or specification changes, if the acquiring party makes adaptations on his own responsibility and without using the technology supplying party's name, trade or service marks or trade names, and except to the extent that this adaptation unsuitably affects those products, or the process for their manufacture, to be supplied to the

/...

Box II.6 (continued)

supplying party, his designates, or his other licensees, or to be used as a component or spare part in a product to be supplied to his customers.

8. Exclusive sales or representation agreements

Requiring the acquiring party to grant exclusive sales or representation rights to the supplying party or any person designated by the supplying party, except as to subcontracting or manufacturing arrangements wherein the parties have agreed that all or part of the production under the technology transfer arrangement will be distributed by the supplying party or any person designated by him.

9. Tying arrangements e/

[Unduly]** imposing acceptance of additional technology, future inventions and improvements, goods or services not wanted by the acquiring party or [unduly]** restricting sources of technology, goods or services, as a condition for obtaining the technology required when not required to maintain the quality of the product or service when the supplier's trade or service mark or other identifying item is used by the acquiring party, or to fulfil a specific performance obligation which has been guaranteed, provided further that adequate specification of the ingredients is not feasible or would involve the disclosure of additional technology not covered by the arrangement.

10. Export restrictions c/

11. Patent pool or cross-licensing agreements and other arrangements

Restrictions on territories, quantities, prices, customers or markets arising out of patent pool or cross-licensing agreements or other international transfer of technology interchange arrangements among technology suppliers which unduly limit access to new technological developments or which would result in an abusive domination of an industry or market with adverse effects on the transfer of technology, except for those restrictions appropriate and ancillary to co-operative arrangements such as co-operative research arrangements.

/...

Box II.6 (concluded)

12. Restrictions on publicity e/

Restrictions [unreasonably]** regulating the advertising or publicity by the acquiring party except where restrictions of such publicity may be required to prevent injury to the supplying party's goodwill or reputation where the advertising or publicity makes reference to the supplying party's name, trade or service marks, trade names or other identifying items, or for legitimate reasons of avoiding product liability when the supplying party may be subject to such liability, or where appropriate for safety purposes or to protect consumers, or when needed to secure the confidentiality of the technology transferred.

13. Payments and other obligations after expiration of industrial property rights

Requiring payments or imposing other obligations for continuing the use of industrial property rights which have been invalidated, cancelled or have expired recognizing that any other issue, including other payment obligations for technology, shall be dealt with by the appropriate applicable law and the terms of the agreement to the extent consistent with that law. f/

14.   Restrictions after expiration of arrangement c/"

Source: UNCTAD, 1996, vol. I, pp. 188-191 and p. 201.

Notes:
a/   In view of the continuing negotiations on the chapter, no attempt has been made to number the provisions of this chapter consistently with other chapters.
b/   Title of chapter 4 under consideration.
c/   For texts under consideration, see appendices A and D.
d/   With regard to practices 15 to 20, see appendix A.1 for text of agreed statement for inclusion in the report of the Conference, and for texts under consideration see appendix D.
e/   Text under consideration. See appendix A.
f/   The spokesmen for the regional groups noted that their acceptance of agreed language which makes reference to the term "applicable law" is conditional upon acceptable resolution of differences in the group texts concerning applicable law and national regulation of this Code.
In the present text, the following key is used to identify the sponsorship of a text, where the text is not an agreed one: Group of 77 text: *; Group B: **; Group D and Mongolia: ***. [Note added by the editor.]

Code. The essence of the disagreement centred on whether certain restrictive terms commonly found in technology licensing agreements should be subjected to a competition law test based on reasonableness, in that such clauses should only be barred where their anti-competitive effects outweighed their pro-competitive effects, or whether they should be banned outright on the grounds that they represented the superior bargaining power of the technology owner and could act against the best interests of the technology recipient. The former position was taken by the major developed countries, while the latter position was championed by the developing countries (Davidow, 2001; Miller and Davidow, 2001; Roffe, 1998; Sell, 2001; and Verma, 2001). On the other hand, there was general agreement over the list of practices that should be subject to regulation. These included grant-back provisions, challenges to validity, exclusive dealing, restrictions on research, restrictions on the use of personnel, price fixing, restrictions on adaptations, exclusive sales or representation agreements, tying arrangements, export restrictions, patent pool or cross-licensing agreements and other arrangements, restrictions on publicity, payments and other obligations after expiration of industrial property rights, and restrictions after expiration of arrangements. However, there remained disagreement on the text relating to some of these practices, namely, export restrictions, publicity restrictions and restrictions after expiration of arrangements.

As can be seen from the developed country position regarding Chapter 4 of the draft TOT Code, the second, market-based approach to RBPs and technology transfer has existed for some time. Indeed, it may be said to have informed the UNCTAD Set of Multilaterally Agreed Equitable Principles and Rules for the Control of Restrictive Business Practices adopted by Resolution 35/63 (1980) of the General Assembly of the United Nations (The Set) (UNCTAD, 1996a, vol. I, p. 133; see further Miller and Davidow, 2001). The Set refers to all kinds of restrictive business practices adversely affecting international trade and economic development of developing countries. One of its objectives is directly related to the transfer of technology to developing countries, namely the attainment of greater efficiency in international trade and development of developing countries through the encouragement of competition and innovation. In addition, certain types of conduct envisaged in the Set may affect the efficacy of transfer of technology transactions, particularly restrictions concerning where, or to whom, or in what form or quantities, goods supplied or other goods may be resold or exported; tying arrangements, whereby the recipient of the technology may be required by the transferor to obtain supplies of other related products or services, or spare parts or other intermediate goods or services, directly from the transferor or their designated supplier; and restrictions on parallel imports.

Moreover, the market-based approach has been used in more recent international instruments, which suggests that the debate that occurred in relation to Chapter 4 of the draft TOT Code has moved in the direction of a competition approach based on the test of the reasonableness of particular restrictive terms and conditions (Roffe and Tesfachew, 2001, p. 397). In particular, under Article 8 (2) of the TRIPS Agreement, States may adopt such measures as may be needed "to prevent the abuse of intellectual property rights by right holders or the resort to practices which unreasonably restrain trade or adversely affect the international transfer of technology" provided that these are consistent with other provisions of the agreement, such as the non-discrimination provisions. This policy is reiterated in Article 40 of the TRIPS Agreement, which provides, as examples of the types of practices that may be controlled, exclusive grant-back conditions, conditions preventing challenges to the validity of IPRs and coercive package licensing. Article 40 adds that members shall enter, on request, into consulations with other members in cases where such abuses of rights are suspected (box II.7).

The NAFTA regime follows a similar approach: Article 1704 of NAFTA specifies that the parties are free to specify, in their domestic law, "licensing practices or conditions that may in particular cases constitute an abuse of intellectual property rights having an adverse effect on competition in the relevant market. A Party may adopt or maintain, consistent with the other provisions of this Agreement, appropriate measures to prevent or control such practices or conditions" (NAFTA, 1993, p. 671).

Box II.7. Agreement on Trade-related Aspects of Intellectual Property Rights

"Article 40

1. Members agree that some licensing practices or conditions pertaining to intellectual property rights which restrain competition may have adverse effects on trade and may impede the transfer and dissemination of technology.

2. Nothing in this Agreement shall prevent Members from specifying in their legislation licensing practices or conditions that may in particular cases constitute an abuse of intellectual property rights having an adverse effect on competition in the relevant market. As provided above, a Member may adopt, consistently with the other provisions of this Agreement, appropriate measures to prevent or control such practices, which may include for example exclusive grantback conditions, conditions preventing challenges to validity and coercive package licensing, in the light of the relevant laws and regulations of that Member.

3. Each Member shall enter, upon request, into consultations with any other Member which has cause to believe that an intellectual property right owner that is a national or domiciliary of the Member to which the request for consultations has been addressed is undertaking practices in violation of the requesting Member's laws and regulations on the subject matter of this Section, and which wishes to secure compliance with such legislation, without prejudice to any action under the law and to the full freedom of an ultimate decision of either Member. The Member addressed shall accord full and sympathetic consideration to, and shall

/...

Furthermore, it should be noted that the OECD Guidelines for Multinational Enterprises recommend that enterprises should, "when granting licences for the use of intellectual property rights or when otherwise transferring technology, do so on reasonable terms and conditions and in a manner that contributes to the long term development prospects of the host country" (Article VIII.4, OECD, 2000, p. 26). Thus, the Guidelines supplement State rights to control RBPs in the field of IPRs with an exhortation that TNCs police their own negotiating practices and avoid the use of unreasonable terms and conditions. Interestingly, the Guidelines go beyond a pure market-based competition analysis and also mention the development prospects of a host country. Though ambiguous as to its precise meaning, this formulation suggests that development concerns may be relevant when determining whether certain terms are reasonable or not. As the Commentary to the Guidelines asserts, not only should TNCs ensure that the terms and conditions on which they sell or license technology

---

Box II.7 (concluded)

afford adequate opportunity for, consultations with the requesting Member, and shall cooperate through supply of publicly available non-confidential information of relevance to the matter in question and of other information available to the Member, subject to domestic law and to the conclusion of mutually satisfactory agreements concerning the safeguarding of its confidentiality by the requesting Member.

4. A Member whose nationals or domiciliaries are subject to proceedings in another Member concerning alleged violation of that other Member's laws and regulations on the subject matter of this Section shall, upon request, be granted an opportunity for consultations by the other Member under the same conditions as those foreseen in paragraph 3."

Source: UNCTAD, 1996a, vol. I, pp. 356-357.

---

are reasonable, but also they may want to consider how they can improve the innovative capacity of their foreign affiliates and subcontractors and add to the local scientific and technological infrastructure, and how they may usefully contribute to the formulation by host governments of policy frameworks conducive to the development of dynamic innovation systems (OECD, 2000; Commentary on Science and Technology, para. 54). Such considerations will no doubt have an impact on what terms and conditions might be regarded as reasonable or unreasonable in the context of a sale or licensing of technology to a recipient in a developing host country.

D. Technology-related host-country measures

As part of their national industrial policy, host countries may impose measures on TNCs designed to further their economic and social policy goals. These measures are the subject of a separate paper in this series (UNCTAD, 2001d). Such measures may be designed *inter alia* to improve the transfer and dissemination of technology into the economy of a host country. Of relevance here may be, for example, employment of foreign professional and technical personnel and training of local personnel requirements; conditions concerning royalty payments; research and development requirements; and transfer of technology requirements.

In relation to this final category, BITs concluded by the United States and, more recently, Canada contain a clause that prohibits performance requirements, including general technology transfer requirements, but which then specifically permits technology transfer requirements where these are imposed by the courts, administrative tribunals or competition authorities of the host contracting party to remedy an alleged violation of competition laws. Examples of such provisions are provided in box II.8.[7]

Box II.8. Technology transfer provisions in BITs

"Article V(2) (e) of the Canada/Philippines BIT of 1995

Neither Contracting Party may impose any of the following requirements in connection with permitting the establishment or acquisition of an investment or enforce any of the following requirements in connection with the subsequent regulation of that investment:

...

(e) to transfer technology, a production process or other proprietary knowledge to a person in its territory unaffiliated with the transferor, except when the requirement is imposed or the commitment or undertaking is enforced by a court, administrative tribunal or competition authority, either to remedy an alleged violation of competition laws, or acting in a manner not inconsistent with the provisions of this Agreement."

"Article VI (e) of the United States Model BIT of 1994

Neither Party shall mandate or enforce, as a condition for the establishment, acquisition, expansion, management, conduct or operation of a covered investment, any requirement (including any commitment or undertaking in connection with the receipt of a governmental permission or authorization):

...

(e) to transfer technology, a production process or other proprietary knowledge to a national or company in the Party's territory, except pursuant to an order, commitment or undertaking that is enforced by a court, administrative tribunal or competition authority to remedy an alleged or adjudicated violation of competition laws;"

Source: UNCTAD, 1998b, pp. 82, 291.

A similar clause is to be found in NAFTA Article 1106 (1) (f), which prohibits any party from imposing or enforcing any commitment related to the establishment, acquisition, expansion management, conduct or operation of an investment on an investor of a party or a

---

non-party in its territory to transfer technology, a production process or other proprietary knowledge to a person in its territory, except when the requirement is imposed or the commitment or undertaking is enforced by a court, administrative tribunal or competition authority to remedy an alleged violation of competition laws or to act in a manner not inconsistent with other provisions of the Agreement (UNCTAD, 1996a, vol. III, p. 75). Article 1106 (2) goes on to exempt, from the prohibition in paragraph (1)(f), any measure that requires an investment to use a technology to meet generally applicable health, safety or environmental requirements, although such measures will be subject to the prohibition on discrimination contained in the national treatment and most-favoured-nation treatment provisions of NAFTA. The NAFTA provisions were followed verbatim in the Canada-Chile Free Trade Agreement of 1996 (Article G-06 (1) (f) and (2), in UNCTAD, 2000b, vol. V, pp. 82-83).

A similar approach to technology transfer requirements was also put forward in the draft MAI provision on performance requirements, although an additional basis for allowing such a performance requirement was offered when such a requirement "concerns the transfer of intellectual property and is undertaken in a manner not inconsistent with the TRIPS Agreement" (UNCTAD, 2000b, vol. IV, pp. 121-122). This formulation was still the subject of discussions at the time the MAI was abandoned. Certain matters remained unresolved, including whether this wording covered future IPRs and moral rights and how this provision would relate to other agreements such as the Rome and Berne Conventions.

The above approach to the issue of technology transfer performance requirements was taken as a starting point for the formulation of a clause on this matter in an alternative International Agreement on Investment prepared by the Consumer Unity and Trust Society (CUTS) of India. Thus Article IV (1) (f) and (2) of this instrument reproduce, in essence, the same provisions as are found in NAFTA and the other agreements mentioned above. However there is one significant difference: Article 4 (7) declares that "Notwithstanding anything contained in paragraph 1, a Contracting Party shall be free to adopt a measure otherwise prohibited by that paragraph for compelling social or economic reasons" (UNCTAD, 2000b, vol. V, p. 420). CUTS explains this proviso by reference to the fact that many countries would find a harsh set of obligations in this area difficult to accept. Furthermore, "a prohibition against requiring a foreign investor to transfer its specialised technology to local citizens would, in effect, mean that the level of technology in the host country would remain stagnant for all times to come. If the host country extends certain benefits, it should, in its turn, be allowed to derive benefits also" (UNCTAD, 2000b, vol. V, p. 421). Thus the CUTS formulation offers an alternative approach based on a degree of regulation that is broader than that accepted by the North American formulation, which restricts regulatory intervention to competition-based or health, safety and environmental technology transfer requirements.

Finally, an alternative formulation, which preserves the full discretion of the host country to impose performance requirements, concerning *inter alia* technology transfer at the point of entry, is provided by the Asian-African Legal Consultative Committee Draft Model Agreement "B" for Promotion and Protection of Investments. Under Article 3(ii) thereof:

> "The investment shall be received subject to the terms and conditions specified in the letter of authorisation. Such terms and conditions may include the obligation or requirement concerning employment of local personnel and labour in the investment projects, organisation of training programmes, transfer of technology and marketing arrangements for the products" (UNCTAD, 1996a, vol. III, p. 129).

This approach is consistent with the regulatory model of technology transfer provisions discussed above.

* * *

This Section has shown that the provisions of IIAs, and related instruments that deal with technology issues, display a shift in focus, offering a range of approaches to such issues. These approaches have been characterized as falling into two main categories: a regulatory model which seeks to control the conditions under which IPRs are protected and technology is transferred, and a market-based development model, which stresses the need to maintain as high a degree of freedom for technology owners to exploit their advantages in this area as they see fit, subject only to competition-based regulation. Furthermore, under this model, host countries are largely restricted in the nature and extent of performance requirements that they might impose in relation to the generation, transfer and diffusion of technology. Of course, these approaches are not mutually incompatible and it is possible to envisage a mixed approach that combines elements of regulation and market freedom. This is the case, it seems, in relation to the treatment of TNC obligations as regards the science and technology policies followed by the countries in which they operate. Furthermore, although competition controls may be seen as part of the market-based development approach, they undoubtedly offer a discretion to host and home countries alike to act with a light or heavy touch in their regulation of the possible anti-competitive effects of technology transactions undertaken by TNCs. The implications of these approaches for the evolution of policy options for the formulation of technology-oriented clauses in IIAs will be further considered, in the context of their possible impacts on development, in Section IV below.

Notes

1   The provisions on IPRs in the North American Free Trade Agreement (NAFTA) are very similar in their principal features to those in the TRIPS Agreement. Accordingly, NAFTA will only be mentioned expressly where this adds to the analysis developed in the light of the TRIPS Agreement. See further NAFTA, 1993.

2   See Case C-355/96 Silhouette vs. Hartlauer (1998), 2, CMLR 953.

3   See IHT Internationale Heiztechnick v. Ideal Standard [1994], 3, Common Market Law Reports 857.

4   In addition to the examples discussed in the text, see also the United Nations Convention on the Law of the Sea 1982 (United Nations Document A/CONF.62/122; reproduced in *International Legal Materials*, 21, 1261 (1982)) which contains extensive provisions on a regulatory regime for the transfer of technology in the fields of, *inter alia*, fisheries, marine scientific research and marine technology generally, including transfers to developing countries and to the Enterprise of the Deep Sea Bed Authority. Certain provisions relating to the transfer of technology were weakened by the 1994 New York Agreement Relating to the Implementation of Part XI of the Law of the Sea Convention in recognition of the need to re?evaluate some aspects of the regime in the light of, in particular, growing reliance on the market.

5   The draft TOT Code states "should act on the basis that these measures should ..."

6   See Framework Agreement for Cooperation Between the EU and the Cartagena Agreement and its Member Countries, 1993, Article 3 (UNCTAD, 2000b, vol. V, p. 187); and EU?MERCOSUR Interregional Framework Co?operation Agreement, 1993, Articles 11(2)and 16(2)(b) (UNCTAD, 2001c, pp. 162-164).

7   On the other hand, the United States/Lithuania BIT of 1998 lacks such a clause. The only reference to prohibited performance requirements concerns export, local purchasing and any other similar requirements (Article II(6)). Technology requirements are not covered by the Agreement.

Section III

INTERACTION WITH OTHER ISSUES AND CONCEPTS

Section III considers the interaction with other issues and concepts. Technology as a cross-cutting issue interacts with most of the concepts in the other papers in this Series. However, it has a more extensive interaction with scope and definition, admission and establishment, standards of treatment, host country operational measures, transfer of funds, competition and the environment. This section will briefly explain these interactions.

Table III.1. Interaction across issues and concepts

Concepts in other papers	Technology transfer
Scope and definition	++
Admission and establishment	++
Incentives	+
Investment-related trade measures	+
Most-favoured-nation treatment	++
National treatment	++
Fair and equitable treatment	++
Taxation	+
Transfer pricing	+
Employment	+
Social responsibility	+
Environment	++
Home country measures	+
Host country operational measures	++
Illicit payments	+
Taking of property	+
State contracts	+
Funds transfer	++
Transparency	+
Competition	++
Dispute settlement (investor-State)	+
Dispute settlement (State-State)	+

Source: UNCTAD.

Key:　0　= negligible or no interaction.
　　　+　= moderate interaction.
　　　++ = extensive interaction.

Scope and definition. Transfers of technology can readily be included in the definition of an investment. This can be done by reference to the assets involved, for example the transfer of IPRs or know-how, or by reference to the underlying transaction. The draft TOT Code used both approaches (see Articles 1.2 and 1.3, in UNCTAD, 1996a, vol. I. p. 183). It also addressed the Code to all parties to transfer of technology transactions and to all countries and groups of countries, irrespective of their economic and political systems and their levels of development (Article 1.5, in UNCTAD, 1996a, vol. I. p. 183). By contrast, the TRIPS Agreement uses an asset-based approach covering all categories of intellectual property that are the subject of the Agreement in Sections 1 to 7 of Part II. These include: copyright and related rights, trademarks, geographical indications, industrial designs, patents, layout designs (topographies) of integrated circuits and undisclosed information. The asset-based approach is also followed in BITs, which usually include a wide definition of IPRs in their scope and application clauses (UNCTAD, 1999b).

Admission and establishment. The interaction between technology and admission and establishment can be considerable. In particular, where a host country has strong review mechanisms for inward FDI it may consider the effect of a particular investment on the generation, transfer and diffusion of technology as a significant part of the review. This may lead to a refusal of entry for the proposed investment where its contribution to these matters is considered to be negligible and there are no other compelling economic or social reasons for granting entry. Alternatively, the host country may admit an investment on certain conditions that require the investor to encourage the generation and/or transfer and/or diffusion of the technology. However, the more recent trend in national laws has been to liberalize conditions of entry and establishment for FDI and so such controls are now less common. Equally, certain BITs and regional investment agreements may prohibit the imposition of technology-related performance requirements, as noted and analysed in Section II.

Standards of treatment. Any requirements for foreign investors as to their obligations in relation to technology issues will raise questions of their compatibility with standards of treatment commonly found in IIAs. Thus, where a host country imposes such requirements, their content, scope and application will have to conform with the national treatment standard, insofar as the treatment of domestic investors engaged in a like activity is concerned, and with the MFN standard, as regards the treatment of other foreign investors engaged in a like activity. Equally, reference to these standards can lead to the prohibition of technology-related requirements on the ground of their incompatibility with the principle of non-discrimination that these standards embody. Indeed, as noted in Section II, such prohibitions are common in certain bilateral and regional agreements.

Environment. The strong interaction between technology transfer and environmental issues was alluded to, and briefly considered, in Section I. That interaction is fully discussed in the paper on the *Environment* in this Series (UNCTAD, 2001b).

Host country operational measures. As noted above in relation to admission and establishment, host countries may impose measures on foreign investors related to technology at the point of entry. Such measures may also be imposed after entry as part of the internal regulation of a host country's economy. In either case the issue of their compatibility with standards of treatment will arise.

Transfer of funds. There is some interaction between technology transfer and the transfer of funds and **taxation** issues as they relate to the payment of, for example, royalties, commissions or lump sums for such transfers. They could be significant and of great relevance to host countries, investors and home countries as when a host country imposes royalty ceilings on technology transfer transactions.

Competition. The interaction between competition and technology issues is now so strong that the latter cannot be discussed in any detail without extensive reference to the former. Thus competition-related questions have been extensively discussed in Section II.

CONCLUSION:

ECONOMIC AND DEVELOPMENT IMPLICATIONS AND POLICY OPTIONS

A. The market for technology and its development implications

Technology, as defined in the Introduction, may be available in non-proprietary forms that can be generally accessed, for example, books or journals. However, the major concern that underlies the regulatory issues covered by the present paper focuses on proprietary technology, that is technology that is capable of generating a profit exclusively for its owner and others who may be able to access it conditionally at a cost. Thus, the first significant feature of the market for commercial technology is that such technology is treated as the private property of its owner and not as a public good available for general use at little or no cost to its user.[1] Commercial technology is usually exploited through the application of intellectual property rights, which give the owner legally determined exclusive rights over the use and disposal of those rights, or by way of protected and restrictive contractual transfer as in the case of non-patentable know-how that is secret, where the contract itself may contain provisions that protect the know-how against abuse by the recipient through the device of restrictive clauses that control the recipient's freedom of action when applying the know-how. This process helps to increase the value of the technology to its owner by creating relative scarcity through legally restricted access to it. However, not all types of useful knowledge are so treated.

The generation and use of commercial technology are closely bound up with the technological infrastructure of a country. This includes the systems and knowledge at the disposal of the public and private organizations that fund the development and adaptation of technology, the public and private R&D organizations that conduct work on new and improved technology, the intermediaries who move the technology around the country and across its borders and the users who apply the technology in their business activities or who are the end consumers of products incorporating the technology in question.[2] Consequently, the states that possess the more developed systems for generating, delivering and using technology are likely to be the leading sources of proprietary technology (UNCTAD, 1999a, pp. 198-202).

TNCs are strongly influential in the operation of national and international technological infrastructures. They can be found operating at each stage of such a system in the most technologically advanced economies of the world. That this should be so stems from the fact that one of the main ownership-specific advantages of TNCs is their ability to "produce, acquire, master the understanding of and organize the use of technological assets across national boundaries".[3] Consequently, TNCs are a major force in shaping international markets for technology, particularly on the supply side. Their influence on the demand side is also significant, given that increasing amounts of international technology transfers occur between related enterprises.

On the supply side, TNCs seek to exploit their proprietary technologies in commercial technology markets for maximum gain; for the world's major TNCs that includes also exploiting their dominant position in such markets. However, the degree of control exercised by these firms may vary according to the type of technology involved.[4] Thus firms operating in more mature technology industries such as footwear, textiles, cement, pulp and paper or food processing may be more willing to transfer their technology than firms operating in high technology areas such as aerospace, electronics, computers, chemicals and machinery. In the latter case, technology owners guard the source of their competitive advantage, making their technology available only on restrictive terms favourable to the earning of a monopoly rent. Furthermore, such considerations may create a preference for internalized transfer of technology within a network of TNC affiliates, rather than an externalized transfer to unaffiliated licensees. However, it would be a mistake to see all "high" technology markets as uncompetitive on the supply side. For example, in some newer high-technology industries, such as semiconductors or computers, the entry of smaller, innovative firms has stimulated choice in sources of technological supply, making for increased competition in that field, although in the long term concentration can be predicted to occur (van Tulder and Junne, 1988, chapter 2). Furthermore, as "high" technology matures into "conventional" technology, new entrants into the field can be expected. The competitive situation on the supply side of a market for technology is not, therefore, a static phenomenon, and each industry should be analysed on its own terms.

The demand side of the market is also conditioned by the nature of the technological infrastructure present in an economy in which a recipient is situated. Thus a distinction can be made between conditions in technologically advanced recipient countries and those in technologically less developed countries (see further Greer, 1981, pp. 56-60). Conditions in the former are characterized by an ability to absorb technology effectively through advanced production systems, a highly trained workforce, high demand for the technology concerned and the ability to pay for it. Furthermore, technologically advanced recipients are often in a stronger position to bargain over the terms of supply. Alternative local sources of technology that can compete with the technology on offer from outside are more likely to exist. Furthermore, there is a greater likelihood that the purchaser will itself be in a strong position to influence the market, as for instance in the case of another major corporation operating at the same level of the market as the supplier, or where it is a producer of competing products, or where it is in a quasi-monopolistic position, for example the postal and telecommunications authority of a major advanced country. In addition, in advanced countries, ensuring the existence of workable competition, even in highly concentrated technology markets, is a principal concern. Thus competition law plays a significant role in the regulation of technology transfers to such countries.

In comparison, the absorption of proprietary technology in countries with a weak technological base is more problematic. The absence of a sophisticated technological infrastructure and a relatively underdeveloped domestic industrial and R&D base have significant consequences for both supply and demand conditions. In particular, there is a high level of dependence on outside suppliers due to the lack of alternative, domestically generated technology. Purchasers are thus in a weak bargaining position which is exacerbated by the relative lack of information about technology caused by the absence of adequate numbers of skilled specialists who could evaluate the technology on offer. In such cases, the technology owner is often likely to enjoy a monopolistic position in relation to the recipient market and may be able to exact excessive prices and restrictions on the utilization of the imported technology.[5]

Furthermore, in these countries, it is less likely that a technology owner can introduce new technology by means other than direct investment through a controlled affiliate. This is because, in general, there are relatively few firms in developing countries that can act as licensees of advanced technology as compared with developed countries. Consequently, the conditions of technology transfer will often be determined by the overall objectives of the TNC as an integrated enterprise. These may be at variance with the interests of the importing economy, particularly to the extent that the transfer and use of technology within and under the control of the firm are less likely to result in its dissemination to potential competitors, if any, in that economy. As commercial enterprises, TNCs in principle do not have an interest in transferring knowledge to and supporting innovation in foreign affiliates beyond what is needed for the production process or product in question. Developing countries therefore cannot expect that, by simply opening their doors to FDI, TNCs will transform their technological base. Conversely, countries could not expect that, by entering IIAs, the transfer of technology process will be facilitated. Deficiencies in technological learning and transfer in developing countries can mean that markets by themselves do not create technological dynamism. At best, they can lead to a better use of static endowments but not to the continuous upgrading that competing in the new context requires. To tap into their potential, host Governments therefore have a role to play in promoting local learning and developing skills and institutions.

On the other hand, more recent research suggests that TNCs may be more willing than in earlier decades to move their technological assets around the world so as to match them with immobile factors, and to forge new alliances and reorganize production relations (UNCTAD, 1999a, pp. 200-201). This could increase opportunities for developing countries to obtain and absorb technologies from other countries and enable at least the more advanced among them to take a more active part in the generation of new technology.

Potentially, TNCs have much to offer in developing local capabilities. What technologies and functions they actually transfer to particular locations, however, depends greatly on local capabilities. There is thus again a role for policy in upgrading capabilities to optimize the transfer of TNC technology and encourage its dissemination. Moreover, there is also a role for policy in attracting higher-quality FDI: providing better information to prospective investors and ensuring that their needs are met can be a vital tool of technology development. However, the new technological and policy context makes it more difficult to promote local technology development. The sheer pace of technological change makes technology strategies more risky and expensive. Not too many developing countries are in a position to create broad and deep domestic capabilities in the immediate future. In the case of developing countries, therefore, especially the least developed, host country efforts need to be complemented by international efforts to foster effective transfer of technology to these countries.

Concerns about the monopolistic tendencies of suppliers in developing country technology markets provided a major justification in the past for calls for greater regulation of international technology transfers in the interests of developing recipient countries. This gave rise to new kinds of legal regimes in the 1970s, based on specialized technology transfer laws, and to negotiations for the above-mentioned international code of conduct on technology transfer under the auspices of UNCTAD. However, the new rules of international trade, investment and the strengthening of protection of intellectual property rights have rendered many instruments used in the past by the then newly industrializing economies more difficult to apply. As regards industrial policy, for instance, it is becoming harder to give infant industry protection or subsidize targeted activities, and local content rules are being phased out. Nevertheless, with regard to technology policy, there is room for developing countries to provide technology support services and finance for innovation. Also, a number of policy options remain to strengthen the "supply side"; the main ones include minimization of business transaction costs, human capital formation, domestic enterprise development, cluster promotion, encouraging closer links between industry and research, and strengthening physical infrastructure. The experience of the developed countries shows that there is, indeed, a wide spectrum of policies that one can pursue to support local entrepreneurship and encourage technological development, especially through the promotion of linkages between foreign affiliates and domestic firms (UNCTAD, 2001a).

B. Policy options

IIAs could play a role in enhancing the generation, transfer and diffusion of technology to developing countries. On the other hand, such agreements could remain silent on technology issues, leaving such matters to national policy makers, other international agreements and international aid programmes subject only to general standards of treatment for foreign investors and their investments.

Against this background, and in the context of the development implications of the international market for technology, a number of policy options present themselves.

Option 1: No coverage of technology issues

This has been the traditional approach to such matters in the overwhelming number of IIAs. As noted in Section II, most BITs do not mention technology as such. Thus, a technology-based transaction, involving the transfer of IPRs, will only be protected by an IIA to the extent that the IPRs in question are included in the definition of protected "investments". In such a case, the only legal effect of the agreement is to ensure that the transaction is given treatment that is in accordance with the international standards of treatment mentioned in the agreement in question.

The advantage of this approach for development is that it does not establish any specific restrictions or responsibilities on the part of a host country in relation to an investor providing the technology other than those standards of treatment already explicitly stated by the IIA. However, the disadvantage is that such an approach does not include any internationally agreed commitments in the agreement for the cooperation of TNCs, or their home Governments, in the promotion of the generation, transfer and diffusion of technology to the host country or for the control of undesirable terms and conditions in technology transfer transactions. Such an outcome could be qualified, however, through the inclusion of a provision along the following lines: "Each Party shall observe any obligation it may have entered into with regard to investments". Such a provision is to be found, for example, in the United States/Jamaica BIT in Article II(2)(C). The effect of such a provision is to incorporate into the BIT any applicable agreements between the Parties on technology transfer, although its original purpose is to render applicable to developing host countries any other obligations they have undertaken in respect of investments.

Option 2: Limited coverage of technology issues: control over technology-related performance requirements

As noted in Section II, some BITs and regional investment agreements only deal with one aspect of technology-related issues, namely the control of technology-related performance requirements. These are prohibited except to the extent that they are based on a competition-related assessment of their economic effects by a judicial, administrative or other authority empowered to make such an assessment.

The principal implication for development is that a host country can only introduce performance requirements in the field of technology which serve to control the competitive conditions of the market in question. This may in itself be good for the economic development of the host country. However, more extensive requirements as to the generation, transfer and diffusion of technology, which go beyond competition-related matters, would be prohibited under this option. Thus, a developing country wishing to employ wider performance requirements, for example local personnel training requirements or the regulation of royalty payments by the technology recipient, may not be able to follow such a strategy should this prohibition exist in the IIA. This suggests a further option.

Option 3: Limited coverage of technology issues: permissible technology transfer requirements

In order to permit greater flexibility for a developing country to introduce certain limited performance requirements in the field of technology transfer, an IIA may include a provision that makes such requirements permissible provided that certain specified policy goals exist. Thus an agreement may make the requirement conditional on the receipt of an advantage to the investor, or on the technology in question being necessary for environmentally sound production. This option assumes, however, that the participating States have not bound themselves under other agreements to prohibit technology-related performance requirements.

One possibility in this regard is to link provisions on technology-related performance requirements with some of the provisions of the OECD Guidelines as regards science and technology, which, as was shown in Section II, contain an acknowledgement that in certain circumstances it may be useful to regulate the conditions of technology transfer to ensure the proper development of the host country's science and technology base. Thus technology-related performance requirements that have as their purpose the development of a host country's science and technology base could be rendered permissible, or indeed, be encouraged by the investment agreement in question.

Option 4: Wide "regulated" coverage of technology issues

This approach was exemplified in section II by the draft TOT Code. The main features of this option are:

*   The modification of the terms of technology transfer transactions to ensure the protection of the technology recipient against abuses of the perceived superior bargaining power of the technology owner. This is done without denial of the validity of the technology owner's rights as an IP holder. Rather, the approach is to control and, where necessary to prohibit, certain clauses in a technology transfer transaction that are deemed incompatible with the weaker bargaining position of the recipient.

*   The recipient's country retains the discretion to impose performance requirements related to the transfer and diffusion of technology upon the transferor.

• The imposition of duties on TNCs and their home Governments actively to adopt policies conducive to the improved generation, transfer and diffusion of technology, especially to developing host countries.

The principal development implication of this option is that it enshrines, in an international instrument, the right of a host country to regulate the conditions of technology transfer and diffusion within its borders as it sees fit in the light of its economic policy priorities. It also creates duties upon TNCs and their home Governments to take positive steps to help developing countries to overcome their disadvantages in the international market for technology by way of obligations to cooperate with such countries and to encourage the increased generation, transfer and diffusion of useful technology to them.

The major disadvantage may be that such a regulated approach to the issue could be perceived as creating commercial disincentives for TNCs, as the principal owners of technology, against the dissemination of that technology to developing host countries. In particular, additional costs may arise as a result of intervention in the bargaining process through protective contractual requirements aimed at the promotion of the interests of independent local technology recipients. The imposition of extensive performance requirements could be perceived as limiting the commercial return on the transfer transaction. This could be possible whether the transfer is effected as an external transfer to a local recipient or as an internal transfer to a local affiliate.

Option 5: Wide "market-based" coverage of technology issues

This option, exemplified in Section II by the TRIPS Agreement in particular, seeks to address the possible commercial disincentives that a strong regulatory approach might create. Thus the emphasis is not so much on the protection of the technology recipient as the weaker bargaining party in a technology transfer transaction, as on the preservation of a free bargaining environment subject mainly to competition considerations. Thus, the main features of this option are:

- A strong reaffirmation of the IPRs of the technology owner, subject only to a limited number of optional constraints based on:

  - The exhaustion of IPRs. Here it should be noted that so far no multilateral agreement has addressed this matter. Regional agreements that have done so do not recognize a general international right of exhaustion; rather, they limit the right to the territory of the regional group in question.

  - Compulsory licensing. Again such provisions are not present in all agreements.

  - Environmental and health concerns. Intervention in the enjoyment of IPRs may be motivated by a need to protect public health and the environment by encouraging the widest possible dissemination of environmentally sound technology based on IPRs which might otherwise remain under the sole control of the technology owner. The paper on *Environment* in this Series deals further with this topic.

- The regulation of the terms of technology transfer transactions based only on competition-related concerns dealing with:

  - The competitive situation of a technology recipient, ensuring that its opportunities to act as an active competitor in the market are not unduly restricted by the technology transferor.

- The competitive position of third parties, ensuring that the technology transferor does not use its dominant position in the market to create barriers to entry for actual and potential competitors, especially through the conclusion of networks of technology licensing agreements with chosen recipients.

• The prohibition of technology-related performance requirements subject to competition considerations as in option 2.

• In common with option 4, a recognition that the international market for technology can act against the interests of developing countries and that, therefore, it is desirable to impose certain obligations on TNCs and their home governments to promote the generation, transfer and diffusion of technology to developing countries. Such obligations can take the form of binding or non-binding recommendations or exhortations to TNCs and/or their home governments.

• A recognition of the special position of developing countries in relation to the impact of full IPR protection on their economies through the inclusion of transitional provisions including, in particular, temporal exemptions from the full obligations to respect the protection of IPRs under national laws and policies.

The development implications of this option are not entirely certain due to the fact that although this option displays considerable faith in the ability of market forces to deliver technology and its attendant advantages to developing countries, provision is nonetheless made for the special position of such countries. Thus this option recognizes that a complete absence of intervention in the market is unlikely to aid the process of technology generation, transfer and diffusion to developing countries.

On the other hand, this approach may encourage such a process by reducing the incidence of extensive regulation in the process of negotiating technology transfers with independent recipients and in the setting up of direct investments involving such transfers. It would therefore be an attractive option for developing countries that wish to open their economies to FDI but also expect a degree of cooperation from TNCs and their home Governments in overcoming the structural disadvantages created by the international market for technology for developing countries.

Option 6: A "hybrid" approach

As noted at the end of Section II, the differences between the regulated and market-based approaches to technology issues may not be very great in practice. A combination of regulatory and market-based provisions may be used in future IIAs dealing with technology questions. An important consideration in this regard concerns the relative legal force to be given to these respective types of clauses: are both regulatory and market-oriented clauses to be legally binding or not? For example, should a duty on the part of TNCs to cooperate in the technology and science policy of the host country, as stated, for example, in the OECD Guidelines for Multinational Enterprises (discussed in Section II), have the same legal force as, say, a prohibition on technology-related performance requirements? There exists here a risk of asymmetrical legal force being given to different aspects of technology-related provisions in IIAs which negotiators should be aware of when considering their position on these matters.

One possible solution, from the perspective of encouraging the development of developing countries, would be to couch the obligation on the part of TNCs to cooperate in the technology and science policy of the developing host country in mandatory language, while provisions prohibiting technology-related performance requirements could be couched in exhortatory "best efforts" language, taking account of the special needs of developing countries.

Option 7: The regional industrial policy approach

As noted in Section II, some regional economic integration organizations among developing countries have adopted special regimes for the generation, transfer and diffusion of technology *inter se*. Such an approach may enhance the opportunities for regional technological development, although much depends on the region's comparative economic advantages. Where this approach ignores foreign investors from outside the region it may risk excluding a significant source of technology. Negotiators must consider carefully the position of such investors in their scheme.

Notes

1   See further Muchlinski, 1999, pp. 427-429, on which the following paragraphs are based.
2   See Anyos, 1979, pp. 195-212. See further van Tulder and Junne, 1988, especially chapters 6 and 7.
3   Dunning, 1992, p. 290. Dunning observed that, in the late 1980s, TNCs were accounting for between 75 per cent and 80 per cent of privately undertaken R&D in the world.
4   See Greer, 1981, p. 48, citing Chudson, 1971, p. 18.
5   See, for an economic analysis of this situation, Rodriguez, 1975.

Appendix
INTERNATIONAL ARRANGEMENTS FOR TRANSFER OF TECHNOLOGY

Outcome of the Expert Meeting

1.   The Expert Meeting on International Arrangements for Transfer of Technology examined a range of issues for consideration by the Commission on Investment, Technology and Related Financial Issues pursuant to paragraphs 117 and 128 of the Bangkok Plan of Action (TD/386).[1]   Experts made presentations and exchanged views on experiences and best practices at the international and national levels.

2.   Experts noted that, in the knowledge-based global economy, technology plays an ever-important role in economic development. The concerns of the international community with respect to enhancing the transfer of technology to developing countries, in particular to the least developed countries, as well as their technological capabilities, are reflected in several dozen international instruments. These instruments express the willingness of development partners to cooperate multilaterally. There has been some success in implementation, but more needs to be done. The availability of information on arrangements for transfer of technology is an essential requirement for sustained multilateral cooperation. In this connection, the *Compendium* on transfer of technology-related provisions[2] is a welcome contribution and should be continuously updated, as necessary, and widely disseminated, including through electronic media.

3.   Experts also noted that most technology-related provisions are of a "best-efforts" nature. Governments, as well as civil society and the private sector, have an important role to play in the implementation of commitments, *inter alia* through public and private partnerships. In

this connection, experts emphasized the importance of adequate protection of intellectual property in providing incentives for investment and transfer of technology in all countries, including in developing countries, taking into account the interests of producers, users and consumers.

4.   Experts examined a number of best practices that can contribute to generating favourable conditions and opportunities for transfer of technology and capacity building. Some of these practices include the following:

(a)   International instruments with built-in implementation mechanisms, including financial provisions and monitoring arrangements, have a promising implementation record and should be emulated. These instruments are relatively few and mainly for purposes of the public good, such as environmental protection. Nevertheless they can serve as a model in other areas such as infrastructure, health, nutrition and telecommunication;

(b)   Ensuring the access, in particular of developing countries, to technological information, including information on state-of-the-art technologies on a competitive basis and on fair and equitable terms and conditions, in addition to information available from the public sources;

(c)   Taking measures to prevent anticompetitive practices by technology rights holders or the resort to practices which unduly impede the transfer and dissemination of technology. Control of such practices is quite common in developed countries, but there is a lack of legislative measures in this regard in many developing countries. In particular, the development of relevant legislation at either the national or regional level is considered to be a promising option;

(d)   Taking into account the possible short and medium-term costs, local working requirements, if applied in a manner that is consistent with the TRIPS Agreement and the Paris Convention, may be one way of enhancing transfer of technology;

(e)   Making the TRIPS Agreement more conducive to transfer of technology, in accordance with its Articles 7, 8 and 40, including by reviewing its impact on transfer of technology and capacity building;

(f)   Setting up of interministerial coordination committees at the national/regional level with regard to the interface between commitments in the TRIPS Agreement and national implementation requirements with a view to adjusting the TRIPS standards to local innovation needs and to favouring their pro-competitive implementation. UNCTAD should assist interested countries in establishing such committees by undertaking a needs assessment in the context of the ongoing programme of science, technology and innovation policy reviews;

(g)   Establishing a special trust fund, based on successful models, to promote research and development in developing countries and other activities in the area of technology with a view to assisting developing countries in benefiting from their various international commitments;

(h)   Designing measures and specific incentives for home-country enterprises, including fiscal and other incentives, to promote transfer of technology, especially through FDI in developing countries. In this connection, the monitoring of implementation of the commitments in Article 66.2 of the TRIPS Agreement could contribute to building a sound and viable technological base in LDCs. UNCTAD should compile an illustrative list of home-country measures that might fulfil the requirements of Article 66.2;

(i) Supporting capacity-building, in particular in LDCs, through specific projects and programmes and by establishing a scientific and technological infrastructure on a cooperative basis for both the public and private research facilities so as to enable them to assess, adopt, manage, apply and improve technologies;

(j) Creating a hospitable domestic regulatory environment for foreign investment, along with intellectual property protection, encourages access to the newest technology. It has been observed that the transfer of technology is often most successful when accomplished by means of investment, specially by FDI. In this connection, technical cooperation should focus on technological capacity building with a view to enabling beneficiary countries to use intellectual property rights properly in ways that advance their national systems of innovation;

(k) Supporting transfer of technology and capacity building for enhancing the use of electronic commerce in developing countries, in particular by their small and medium sized enterprises, including enhancing the use of information and technologies in the public domain;

(l) The provision by host countries of an enabling environment for transfer of technology, taking into account the following considerations:

- Vocational training and recruitment of technical staff;
- Relationships with local public or private research centres and consultancy firms;
- Joint efforts by enterprises and Governments;

-   Encouraging capacity building for assessing, adopting, managing, and applying technologies through *inter alia*: human resources development, strengthening institutional capacities for research and development and programme implementation, assessments of technology needs, and long-term technological partnerships between holders of technologies and potential local users.

5.   UNCTAD should provide assistance to developing countries, in particular least developed countries, to strengthen their capacity for discussing and for negotiating technology transfer provisions in international instruments. UNCTAD should further explore ways and means for effective implementation of international commitments in the area of transfer of technology and capacity building.

Notes

[1]   Paragraph 117: "UNCTAD should analyse all aspects of existing international agreements relevant to transfer of technology". Paragraph 128: "In the area of transfer of technology, UNCTAD should examine and disseminate widely information on best practices for access to technology".
[2]   Compendium of International Arrangements on Transfer of Technology: Selected Instruments (UNCTAD/ITE/IPC/Misc.5).

Annex table 1. Technology transfer obligations under certain multilateral environment agreements (MEAs)

MEA	MEA objective	Obligation on State relevant to technology transfer
Basel Convention	To eliminate, as far as practicable, the generation of hazardous wastes and other wastes and to promote the sound management of hazardous wastes produced locally	*Article 10(2)(d)* The Parties shall cooperate actively, subject to their national laws, regulations and policies, in the transfer of technology and management systems related to the environmentally sound management of hazardous wastes and other wastes.
Rotterdam Convention on the Prior Informed Consent Procedure for Certain Hazardous Chemicals and Pesticides in International Trade	To address the need to strengthen national capabilities and capacities for the management of chemicals	*Preamble* of Annex III: Taking into account the circumstances and particular requirements of developing countries [...], in particular the need to strengthen national capabilities for the management of chemicals, including transfer of technology, providing financial assistance and promoting cooperation among the Parties. *Article 14(1)* The Parties shall facilitate the exchange of information [...] including toxicological, ecotoxicological and safety information. *Article 14(2)* The Parties [...] shall protect any confidential information as mutually agreed.
Vienna Convention	To protect and replenish the ozone layer by eliminating the production and use of ozone-depleting substances	*Article 4(2)* The Parties shall co-operate, consistent with their national laws, regulations and practices, taking into account in particular the needs of the developing countries, in promoting, directly or through competent international bodies, the development and transfer of technology and knowledge. *Article 4(1)* The Parties shall facilitate and encourage the exchange of [...] information. [...] Any such body receiving information regarded as

/...

MEA	MEA objective	Obligation on State relevant to technology transfer
		confidential by the supplying Party shall ensure that such information is not disclosed and shall aggregate it to protect its confidentiality before it is made available to all Parties.
Montreal Protocol - London Amendments	To control, reduce or phase out emissions of substances that deplete the ozone layer	*Article 10A* Each Party shall take every practicable step, consistent with the programmes supported by the financial mechanism, to ensure that the best available, environmentally safe substitutes and related technologies are expeditiously transferred to [...] [developing countries] under fair and most favorable conditions.
Climate Change Convention	To stabilize greenhouse gas concentrations in the atmosphere at a level that would prevent dangerous anthropogenic interference with the climate system	*Article 4(5)* Developed country Parties [...] shall take all practicable steps to promote, facilitate and finance, as appropriate, the transfer of, or access to, environmentally sound technologies and know-how to other Parties, particularly developing country Parties, to enable them to implement the provisions of the Convention. [...] Developed country Parties shall support the development and enhancement of endogenous capacities and technologies of developing country Parties. [...]
Kyoto Protocol	To mitigate climate change (see objectives of the Climate Change Convention)	*Article 10(c)* To cooperate in the promotion of effective modalities for the development, application and diffusion of, and take all practicable steps to promote, facilitate and finance, as appropriate, the transfer of, or access to, environmentally sound technologies, know-how, practices and processes pertinent to climate change, in particular to developing countries, including the formulation of policies and programmes for the effective transfer of environmentally sound technologies [...] and the creation of

/...

MEA	MEA objective	Obligation on State relevant to technology transfer
		an enabling environment for the private sector to promote and enhance the transfer of, and access to, environmentally sound technologies.
London Guidelines	To protect human health and the environment	*Article 13(a)(i)* States should facilitate the exchange of information [...] concerning the management of chemicals, particularly through designated national governmental authorities and through intergovernmental organizations as appropriate. *Article 11(a)* States undertaking information exchange [...] should establish internal procedures for the receipt, handling and protection of confidential and proprietary information received from other States.
Desertification Convention	To combat desertification and mitigate the effects of drought, particularly in Africa	*Article 18(1)(b)* The Parties shall facilitate access to technology, in particular by affected developing country Parties, on favorable terms, including on concessional and preferential terms, as mutually agreed, [...] to technologies most suitable to practical application for specific needs of local populations, paying special attention to the social, cultural, economic and environmental impact of such technology.
Tropical Timber Agreement	To provide an effective framework for consultation, international cooperation and policy development among all members with regard to all relevant aspects of the world timber economy. To promote cooperation between members as partners in development reforestation, rehabilitation and forest management activities	*Chapter I - Objectives Article 1 (m)* To promote the access to, and transfer of, technologies and technical cooperation to implement the objectives of this Agreement, including on concessional and preferential terms and conditions, as mutually agreed.

/...

MEA	MEA objective	Obligation on State relevant to technology transfer
Industrial Accidents Convention	To prevent, prepare for and respond to the effects of industrial accidents capable of causing transboundary effects	*Article 16.1 (a)* The Parties shall, consistent with their national laws, [...] facilitate the exchange of technology for the prevention of, preparedness for and response to the effects of industrial accidents, particularly through the exchange of available technology on various financial bases. *Article 22* The provisions of this Convention shall not affect the rights or the obligations of Parties [...] to protect information related to personal data, industrial and commercial secrecy, including intellectual property, or national security.

Source: Based on tables that appeared in unpublished UNEP papers prepared by the Center for International Environmental Law, Geneva, in 1999 and 2000.

References

Andean Community (2000). "Decision 486 on the common intellectual property regime", 1 December. http://www.comunidadandina. org/english/dec/d486e.htm.

Anyos, T. (1979). "Mechanisms for technology transfer: the role of the infrastructure", in S.Gee (ed.), *Technology Transfer in Industrialized Countries* (Amsterdam: Sijthoff), pp. 195-212.

Beier, Friedrich-Karl (1980). "The significance of the patent system for technical, economic and social progress", *International Review of Industrial Property and Copyright Law*, 11, 563, pp. 563-584.

Blakeney, M. (1989). *Legal Aspects of Technology Transfer to Developing Countries* (Oxford: ESC Publishing).

Chudson, W. (1971). *The International Transfer of Commercial Technology to Developing Countries* (New York: UNITAR).

Davidow, Joel (2001). "Stalemate in the negotiations on restrictive practices", in S. J. Patel, P. Roffe and A. Yusuf (eds.), *International Technology Transfer: The Origins and Aftermath of the United Nations Negotiations on a Draft Code of Conduct* (London, The Hague and Boston: Kluwer Law International), pp. 209-215.

Dunning, John H. (1992). *Multinational Enterprises and the Global Economy* (Workingham, England: Addison-Wesley).

_____ (1997). *Alliance Capitalism and Global Business* (London: Routledge).

European Commission (EC) (2000). *Partnership Agreement between the Members of the African, Caribbean and Pacific Group of States of the one part, and the European Community and its Member States, of the other part, signed in Cotonou, Benin on 23 June 2000.* http://www.acpsec.org/gb/cotonou/accord1e.htm.

Ferrantino, M. J. (1993). "The effect of intellectual property rights on international trade and investment", *Weltwirtschaftliches Archiv,* 129, 2, pp. 300-331.

Greer, D. (1981). "Control of terms and conditions for international transfers of technology to developing countries", in O. Schachter and R. Hellawell (eds.), *Competition in International Business* (New York: Columbia University Press), pp. 41-83.

Haines Ferrari, Martha (2000). *The Mercosur Codes* (London: British Institute of International and Comparative Law).

Helleiner, G. K. (1975). "The role of multinational corporations in the less developed countries' trade in technology", *World Development,* 3, pp. 161-189.

_____ (1977). "International technology issues: Southern needs and Northern responses", in J.Bhagwati (ed.), *The New International Economic Order: The North-South Debate* (New York: MIT Press), pp. 295-316.

International Legal Materials (ILM) (1992). "United Nations Conference on Environment and Development: Convention on Biological Diversity", *International Legal Materials,* 31, 4, pp. 818-841.

Kondo, Edson K. (1995). "The effect of patent protection on foreign direct investment", *Journal of World Trade,* 29, 6 (December), pp. 97-122.

Mansfield, Edwin (1994) "Intellectual property protection, foreign direct investment and technology transfer", *World Bank Discussion Paper,* No. 19 (Washington, DC: World Bank and International Finance Corporation).

_____ (1995). "Intellectual property protection, direct investment and technology transfer: Germany, Japan and the United States", *World Bank Discussion Paper,* No. 27 (Washington, DC: World Bank and International Finance Corporation).

Maskus, Keith E. (2000). *Intellectual Property Rights in the Global Economy* (Washington, DC: Institute for International Economics).

_____ and Yang, Guifang (2000). "Intellectual property rights, foreign direct investment and competition issues in developing countries", *International Journal of Technology Management*, 19, 1-2, pp. 22-34.

Miller, Debra L. and Joel Davidow (2001). "Antitrust at the United Nations: a tale of two codes" in S. J. Patel, P. Roffe and A. Yusuf (eds.), *International Technology Transfer: The Origins and Aftermath of the United Nations Negotiations on a Draft Code of Conduct* (London, The Hague and Boston: Kluwer Law International), pp. 77-102.

Minta, Ike K. (1990). "Intellectual property rights and investment issues in the Uruguay Round", *CTC Reporter,* 29 (Spring), pp. 43-46.

Muchlinski, Peter T. (1999). *Multinational Enterprises and the Law* (Oxford: Blackwell Publishers), 2nd edition.

National Law Center for Inter-American Free Trade (NLC) (1998). *Registro Oficial (Paraguay): Law 912, which approves the Harmonization Protocol of Norms on Intellectual Property in the MERCOSUR, regarding Trademarks, Indications of Source and Denominations of Origin.* http://www.natlaw.com/paraguay/trans/tstprip3.htm.

North American Free Trade Agreement (NAFTA) (1993). "North American Free Trade Agreement", *International Legal Materials,* 32, pp. 605-799.

Omer, Assad (2001). "An overview of legislative changes", in S. J. Patel, P. Roffe and A. Yusuf (eds.), *International Technology Transfer: The Origins and Aftermath of the United Nations Negotiations on a Draft Code of Conduct* (London, The Hague and Boston: Kluwer Law International), pp. 295-312.

Organisation for Economic Co-operation and Development (OECD) (2000). *The OECD Guidelines for Multinational Enterprises* (Paris: OECD).

Patel, S. J., P. Roffe and A. Yusuf (eds.) (2001), *International Technology Transfer: The Origins and Aftermath of the United Nations Negotiations on a Draft Code of Conduct* (London, The Hague and Boston: Kluwer Law International).

Reddy, Prasada (2000). *The Globalisation of Corporate R&D: Implications for Innovation Systems in Host Countries* (London: Routledge).

Rodriguez, Carlos Alfredo (1975). "Trade in technological knowledge and the national advantage", *Journal of Political Economy,* 83, 121, pp. 121-135.

Roffe, Pedro (1998). "Control of anti-competitive practice in contractual licenses under the TRIPS Agreement", in C. Correa and A. A. Yusuf (eds.), *Intellectual Property Rights and International Trade: The TRIPS Agreement* (London, The Hague and Boston: Kluwer Law International), pp. 261-296.

_____ (2000). "The political economy of intellectual property rights: an historical perspective", in Julio Faundez, Mary E. Footer and Joseph J.Norton (eds.), *Governance Development and Globalization* (London: Blackstone Press), pp. 397-413.

_____ and T. Tesfachew (2001), "The unfinished agenda", in S. J. Patel, P. Roffe and A. Yusuf (eds.), *International Technology Transfer: The Origins and Aftermath of the United Nations Negotiations on a Draft Code of Conduct*

(London, The Hague and Boston: Kluwer Law International), pp. 381-404.

Santikarn, Miagsam (1981). *Technology Transfer* (Singapore: Singapore University Press).

Sell, Susan (2001). "Negotiations on an international code of conduct for the transfer of technology", in S. J. Patel, P. Roffe and A. Yusuf (eds.), *International Technology Transfer: The Origins and Aftermath of the United Nations Negotiations on a Draft Code of Conduct* (London, The Hague and Boston: Kluwer Law International), pp. 151-175.

Trebilcock, Michael J. and Robert Howse (1999). *The Regulation of International Trade* (London: Routledge), 2nd edition.

Ubezonu, C. (1990). "The law, policy and practice of technology transfer to Nigeria", PhD Thesis, University of London, mimeo..

United Nations Conference on Trade and Development (UNCTAD) (1985). "Draft International Code of Conduct on the Transfer of Technology, as at the close of the sixth session of Conference on 5 June 1985" (Geneva: United Nations), United Nations document, No.TD/CODE TOT/47, 20 June.

_____ (1996a). *International Investment Instruments: A Compendium,* three volumes (Geneva: United Nations), United Nations publications, Sales Nos. E.96.II.A.9; E.96.II.A.10; and E.96.II.A.11.

_____ (1996b). *The TRIPS Agreement and Developing Countries* (New York and Geneva: United Nations), United Nations publication, Sales No. E.96.II.D.10.

_____ (1998a). *Foreign Direct Investment and Development. UNCTAD Series on Issues in International Investment Agreements* (Geneva: United Nations), United Nations publication, Sales No. E.98.II.D.15.

_____ (1998b) *Bilateral Investment Treaties in the mid-1990s* (Geneva: United Nations), United Nations publication, Sales No. E.98.II.D.8.

_____ (1999a). *World Investment Report 1999: Foreign Direct Investment and the Challenge of Development* (Geneva: United Nations), United Nations publication, Sales No. E.99.II.D.3.

_____ (1999b). *Scope and Definition. UNCTAD Series on Issues in International Investment Agreements* (Geneva: United Nations), United Nations publication, Sales No. E.99.II.D.9.

_____ (1999c). *Lessons from the MAI. UNCTAD Series on Issues in International Investment Agreements* (Geneva: United Nations), United Nations publication, Sales No. E.99.II.D.23.

_____ (2000a). *World Investment Report 2000: Cross-border Mergers and Acquisitions and Development* (Geneva: United Nations), United Nations publication, Sales No. E.00.II.D.20.

_____ (2000b). *International Investment Instruments: A Compendium,* vols. IV and V (Geneva: United Nations), United Nations publications, Sales Nos. E.00.II.D.13 and E.00.II.D.14.

_____ (2001a). *World Investment Report 2001: Promoting Linkages* (Geneva: United Nations), United Nations publication, Sales No. E.01.II.D.12.

_____ (2001b). *Environment. UNCTAD Series on Issues in International Investment Agreements* (Geneva: United Nations), United Nations publication, Sales No. E.01.II.D.3.

_____ (2001c). *Compendium of International Arrangements on Transfer of Technology: Selected Instruments* (Geneva: United Nations), United Nations publication, Sales No. E.01.II.D.28.

_____ (2001d). *Host Country Operational Measures. UNCTAD Series on Issues in International Investment Agreements* (Geneva: United Nations), United Nations publication, Sales No. E.01.II.D.18.

United Nations, Transnational Corporations and Management Division (UNTCMD) (1993). *Intellectual Property Rights and Foreign Direct Investment* (New York: United Nations), United Nations publication, Sales No. E.93.II.A.10.

Van Tulder, R. and G. Junne (1988). *European Multinationals in Core Technologies* (Chichester, New York: Wiley/IRM).

Verma, S. K. (2001). "The TRIPS Agreement and development", in S. J. Patel, P. Roffe and A. Yusuf (eds.), *International Technology Transfer: The Origins and Aftermath of the United Nations Negotiations on a Draft Code of Conduct* (London, The Hague and Boston: Kluwer Law International), pp. 321-350.

Selected UNCTAD publications on transnational corporations and foreign direct investment

A. IIA Issues Paper Series

Illicit Payments. UNCTAD Series on Issues in International Investment Agreements. 114 p. Sales No. E.01.II.D.20.

Home Country Measures. UNCTAD Series on Issues in International Investment Agreements. 101 p. Sales No. E.01.II.D.19.

Social Responsibility. UNCTAD Series on Issues in International Investment Agreements. 91 p. Sales No. E.01.II.D.4.

Environment. UNCTAD Series on Issues in International Investment Agreements. 105 p. Sales No. E.01.II.D.3. $15.

Transfer of Funds. UNCTAD Series on Issues in International Investment Agreements. 68 p. Sales No. E.00.II.D.27. $12.

Employment. UNCTAD Series on Issues in International Investment Agreements. 58 p. Sales No. E.00.II.D.15. $10.

International Investment Agreements: Flexibility for Development. UNCTAD Series on Issues in International Investment Agreements. 170 p. Sales No. E.00.II.D.6. $12.

Taxation. UNCTAD Series on Issues in International Investment Agreements. 100 p. Sales No. E.00.II.D.5. $12.

Taking of Property. UNCTAD Series on Issues in International Investment Agreements. 75p. Sales No. E.00.II.D.4. $12.

Trends in International Investment Agreements: An Overview. UNCTAD Series on Issues in International Investment Agreements. 123 p. Sales No. E.99.II.D.23. $12.

Lessons from the MAI. UNCTAD Series on Issues in International Investment Agreements. 31p. Sales No. E.99.II.D.26. $12.

National Treatment. UNCTAD Series on Issues in International Investment Agreements. 75p. Sales No. E.99.II.D.16. $12.

Fair and Equitable Treatment. UNCTAD Series on Issues in International Investment Agreements. 66 p. Sales No. E.99.II.D.15. $12.

Investment-Related Trade Measures. UNCTAD Series on Issues in International Investment Agreements. 64 p. Sales No. E.99.II.D.12. $12.

Most-Favoured-Nation Treatment. UNCTAD Series on Issues in International Investment Agreements. 72 p. Sales No. E.99.II.D.11. $12.

Admission and Establishment. UNCTAD Series on Issues in International Investment Agreements. 72 p. Sales No. E.99.II.D.10. $12. English and French.

Scope and Definition. UNCTAD Series on Issues in International Investment Agreements. 96p. Sales No. E.99.II.D.9. $12.

Transfer Pricing. UNCTAD Series on Issues in International Investment Agreements. 72 p. Sales No. E.99.II.D.8. $12.

Foreign Direct Investment and Development. UNCTAD Series on Issues in International Investment Agreements. 88 p. Sales No. E.98.II.D.15. $12

B. Individual studies

World Investment Report 2001: Promoting Linkages. 385 p. Sales No. E.01.II.D.12. $45.

World Investment Report 2001: Promoting Linkages. An Overview. 73 p. Free-of-charge.

Measures of the Transnationalization of Economic Activity. 93p. UNCTAD/ITE/IIA/1. Sales No. E.01.II.D.2. $20.

The Competitiveness Challenge: Transnational Corporations and Industrial Restructuring in Developing Countries. 283p. UNCTAD/ITE/IIT/ Misc.20. Sales No. E.00.II.D.35. $42.

Investment Policy Review of Mauritius. 84 p. UNCTAD/ITE/IPC/ Misc.1. Sales No. E.01.II.D.11. $22.

Investment Policy Review of Peru. 108 p. UNCTAD/ITE/IPC/ Misc.19. Sales No. E.00.II.D. 7. $22.

Investment Policy Review of Ecuador. 117 p. UNCTAD/ITE/IPC/ Misc.2.

Investment Policy Review of Ethiopia. 117 p. UNCTAD/ITE/IPC/ Misc.4.

Tax Incentives and Foreign Direct Investment: A Global Survey. ASIT Advisory Studies, No.16. 180p.UNCTAD/ITE/IPC/Misc.3. $23.

Investment Regimes in the Arab World Issues and Policies. ASIT Advisory Studies, No.15. 232p. UNCTAD/ITE/IIP/Misc.21. $39.

The Role of Publicly Funded Research and Publicly Owned Technologies in the Transfer and Diffusion of Environmentally Sound Technologies. 445 p. Sales No. E.00.II.D.37. $45.

Bilateral Investment Treaties 1959-1999. 136 p. UNCTAD/ITE/ IIA/2. 143p. Also available on the internet, http://www.unctad.org/en/ pub/poiteiiad2.en.htm. Free-of-charge.

World Investment Report 2000: Cross-border Mergers and Acquisitions and Development. 337 p. Sales No. E.00.II.D.20. $49 and $19.

World Investment Report 2000: Cross-border Mergers and Acquisitions and Development. An Overview. 65 p. Free-of-charge.

FDI Determinants and TNCs Strategies: The Case of Brazil. 195 p. Sales No. E.00.II.D.2. $35.

International Investment Instruments: A Compendium. Vol. IV. 298 p.; Vol. V. 473 p. Sales Nos. E.00.II.D.13 and E.00.II.D.14. $60 and $42.

Guide d'investissement au Mali. September 2000. UNCTAD/ITE/ IIT/Misc.23 (Joint publication with the International Chamber of Commerce). Free-of-charge.

An Investment Guide to Bangladesh: Opportunities and Conditions, August 2000. UNCTAD/ITE/IIT/Misc.29 (Joint publication with the International Chamber of Commerce). Free-of-charge.

An Investment Guide to Ehiopia: Opportunities and Conditions, April 2000. UNCTAD/ITE/IIT/Misc.19 (Joint publication with the International Chamber of Commerce). Free-of-charge.

World Investment Directory. Vol. VII: Asia and the Pacific 2000. Part 1. 332 p.; Part 2. 305 p. Sales No. E.00.II.D.11. $80.

World Investment Report 1999: Foreign Direct Investment and the Challenge of Development. 536 p. Sales No. E.99.II.D.3. $ 45.

World Investment Report 1999: Foreign Direct Investment and the Challenge of Development. An Overview. 75 p. Free-of-charge.

Investment Policy Review of Uganda. 75 p. Sales No. E.99.II.D.24. $15.

Investment Policy Review of Egypt. 113 p. Sales No. E.99.II.D.20. $19.

Science, Technology and Innovation Policy Review of Colombia. 175 p. Sales No. E.99.II.D.13. $23.

Science, Technology and Innovation Policy Review of Jamaica. 172 p. Sales No. E.98.II.D.7. $42.

Foreign Direct Investment in Africa: Performance and Potential. 89 p. UNCTAD/ITE/IIT/Misc. 15.

Investment Policy Review of Uzbekistan. 64 p. UNCTAD/ITE/IIP/ Misc. 13. Free-of-charge.

The Financial Crisis in Asia and Foreign Direct Investment: An Assessment. 101 p. Sales No. GV.E.98.0.29. $20.

World Investment Report 1998: Trends and Determinants. 430 p. Sales No. E.98.II.D.5. $45.

World Investment Report 1998: Trends and Determinants. An Overview. 67 p. Free-of-charge.

Bilateral Investment Treaties in the mid-1990s. 314 p. Sales No. E.98.II.D.8. $46.

Handbook on Foreign Direct Investment by Small and Medium-sized Enterprises: Lessons from Asia. 200 p. Sales No. E.98.II.D.4. $48.

Handbook on Foreign Direct Investment by Small and Medium-sized Enterprises: Lessons from Asia. Executive Summary and Report on the Kunming Conference. 74 p. Free-of-charge.

International Investment Towards the Year 2002. 166 p. Sales No. GV.E.98.0.15. $29. (Joint publication with Invest in France Mission and Arthur Andersen, in collaboration with DATAR.)

World Investment Report 1997: Transnational Corporations, Market Structure and Competition Policy. 420 p. Sales No. E.97.II.D.10. $45.

World Investment Report 1997: Transnational Corporations, Market Structure and Competition Policy. An Overview. 70 p. Free-of-charge.

International Investment Towards the Year 2001. 81 p. Sales No. GV.E.97.0.5. $35. (Joint publication with Invest in France Mission and Arthur Andersen, in collaboration with DATAR.)

World Investment Directory. Vol. VI: West Asia 1996. 192 p. Sales No. E.97.II.A.2. $35.

World Investment Directory. Vol. V: Africa 1996. 508 p. Sales No. E.97.II.A.1. $75.

Sharing Asia's Dynamism: Asian Direct Investment in the European Union. 192 p. Sales No. E.97.II.D.1. $26.

Transnational Corporations and World Development. 656 p. ISBN 0-415-08560-8 (hardback), 0-415-08561-6 (paperback). $65 (hardback), $20 (paperback). (Published by International Thomson Business Press on behalf of UNCTAD.)

Companies without Borders: Transnational Corporations in the 1990s. 224 p. ISBN 0-415-12526-X. $47.50. (Published by International Thomson Business Press on behalf of UNCTAD.)

The New Globalism and Developing Countries. 336 p. ISBN 92-808-0944-X. $25. (Published by United Nations University Press.)

Investing in Asia's Dynamism: European Union Direct Investment in Asia. 124 p. ISBN 92-827-7675-1. ECU 14. (Joint publication with the European Commission.)

World Investment Report 1996: Investment, Trade and International Policy Arrangements. 332 p. Sales No. E.96.II.A.14. $45.

World Investment Report 1996: Investment, Trade and International Policy Arrangements. An Overview. 51 p. Free-of-charge.

International Investment Instruments: A Compendium. Vol. I. 371 p. Sales No. E.96.II.A.9; Vol. II. 577 p. Sales No. E.96.II.A.10; Vol. III. 389 p. Sales No. E.96.II.A.11; the 3-volume set, Sales No. E.96.II.A.12. $125.

World Investment Report 1995: Transnational Corporations and Competitiveness. 491 p. Sales No. E.95.II.A.9. $45.

World Investment Report 1995: Transnational Corporations and Competitiveness. An Overview. 51 p. Free-of-charge.

Accounting for Sustainable Forestry Management. A Case Study. 46 p. Sales No. E.94.II.A.17. $22.

Small and Medium-sized Transnational Corporations. Executive Summary and Report of the Osaka Conference. 60 p. Free-of-charge.

World Investment Report 1994: Transnational Corporations, Employment and the Workplace. 482 p. Sales No. E.94.II.A.14. $45.

World Investment Report 1994: Transnational Corporations, Employment and the Workplace. An Executive Summary. 34 p. Free-of-charge.

Liberalizing International Transactions in Services: A Handbook. 182 p. Sales No. E.94.II.A.11. $45 (Joint publication with the World Bank.)

World Investment Directory. Vol. IV: Latin America and the Caribbean. 478 p. Sales No. E.94.II.A.10. $65.

Conclusions on Accounting and Reporting by Transnational Corporations. 47 p. Sales No. E.94.II.A.9. $25.

Accounting, Valuation and Privatization. 190 p. Sales No. E.94.II.A.3. $25.

Environmental Management in Transnational Corporations: Report on the Benchmark Corporate Environment Survey. 278 p. Sales No. E.94.II.A.2. $29.95.

Management Consulting: A Survey of the Industry and Its Largest Firms. 100 p. Sales No. E.93.II.A.17. $25.

Transnational Corporations: A Selective Bibliography, 1991-1992. 736 p. Sales No. E.93.II.A.16. $75. (English/French.)

Small and Medium-sized Transnational Corporations: Role, Impact and Policy Implications. 242 p. Sales No. E.93.II.A.15. $35.

World Investment Report 1993: Transnational Corporations and Integrated International Production. 290 p. Sales No. E.93.II.A.14. $45.

World Investment Report 1993: Transnational Corporations and Integrated International Production. An Executive Summary. 31 p. ST/CTC/159. Free-of-charge.

Foreign Investment and Trade Linkages in Developing Countries. 108 p. Sales No. E.93.II.A.12. $18.

World Investment Directory 1992. Vol. III: Developed Countries. 532 p. Sales No. E.93.II.A.9. $75.

Transnational Corporations from Developing Countries: Impact on Their Home Countries. 116 p. Sales No. E.93.II.A.8. $15.

Debt-Equity Swaps and Development. 150 p. Sales No. E.93.II.A.7. $35.

From the Common Market to EC 92: Regional Economic Integration in the European Community and Transnational Corporations. 134 p. Sales No. E.93.II.A.2. $25.

World Investment Directory 1992. Vol. II: Central and Eastern Europe. 432 p. Sales No. E.93.II.A.1. $65. (Joint publication with the United Nations Economic Commission for Europe.)

The East-West Business Directory 1991/1992. 570 p. Sales No. E.92.II.A.20. $65.

World Investment Report 1992: Transnational Corporations as Engines of Growth: An Executive Summary. 30 p. Sales No. E.92.II.A.24. Free-of-charge.

World Investment Report 1992: Transnational Corporations as Engines of Growth. 356 p. Sales No.E.92.II.A.19. $45.

World Investment Directory 1992. Vol. I: Asia and the Pacific. 356 p. Sales No. E.92.II.A.11. $65.

Climate Change and Transnational Corporations: Analysis and Trends. 110 p. Sales No. E.92.II.A.7. $16.50.

Foreign Direct Investment and Transfer of Technology in India. 150 p. Sales No. E.92.II.A.3. $20.

The Determinants of Foreign Direct Investment: A Survey of the Evidence. 84 p. Sales No. E.92.II.A.2. $12.50.

The Impact of Trade-Related Investment Measures on Trade and Development: Theory, Evidence and Policy Implications. 108 p. Sales No. E.91.II.A.19. $17.50. (Joint publication with the United Nations Centre on Transnational Corporations.)

Transnational Corporations and Industrial Hazards Disclosure. 98 p. Sales No. E.91.II.A.18. $17.50.

Transnational Business Information: A Manual of Needs and Sources. 216 p. Sales No. E.91.II.A.13. $45.

World Investment Report 1991: The Triad in Foreign Direct Investment. 108 p. Sales No.E.91.II.A.12. $25.

C. Serial publications

Current Studies, Series A

No. 30. *Incentives and Foreign Direct Investment.* 98 p. Sales No. E.96.II.A.6. $30. (English/French.)

No. 29. *Foreign Direct Investment, Trade, Aid and Migration.* 100 p. Sales No. E.96.II.A.8. $25. (Joint publication with the International Organization for Migration.)

No. 28. *Foreign Direct Investment in Africa.* 119 p. Sales No. E.95.II.A.6. $20.

No. 27. *Tradability of Banking Services: Impact and Implications.* 195 p. Sales No. E.94.II.A.12. $50.

No. 26. *Explaining and Forecasting Regional Flows of Foreign Direct Investment.* 58 p. Sales No. E.94.II.A.5. $25.

No. 25. *International Tradability in Insurance Services.* 54 p. Sales No. E.93.II.A.11. $20.

No. 24. *Intellectual Property Rights and Foreign Direct Investment.* 108 p. Sales No. E.93.II.A.10. $20.

No. 23. *The Transnationalization of Service Industries: An Empirical Analysis of the Determinants of Foreign Direct Investment by Transnational Service Corporations.* 62 p. Sales No. E.93.II.A.3. $15.

No. 22. *Transnational Banks and the External Indebtedness of Developing Countries: Impact of Regulatory Changes.* 48 p. Sales No. E.92.II.A.10. $12.

No. 20. *Foreign Direct Investment, Debt and Home Country Policies.* 50 p. Sales No. E.90.II.A.16. $12.

No. 19. *New Issues in the Uruguay Round of Multilateral Trade Negotiations.* 52 p. Sales No. E.90.II.A.15. $12.50.

No. 18. *Foreign Direct Investment and Industrial Restructuring in Mexico.* 114 p. Sales No. E.92.II.A.9. $12.

No. 17. *Government Policies and Foreign Direct Investment.* 68 p. Sales No. E.91.II.A.20. $12.50.

The United Nations Library on Transnational Corporations
(Published by Routledge on behalf of the United Nations.)

Set A (Boxed set of 4 volumes. ISBN 0-415-08554-3. ,350):
Volume One: The Theory of Transnational Corporations. 464 p.
Volume Two: Transnational Corporations: A Historical Perspective. 464 p.
Volume Three: Transnational Corporations and Economic Development. 448 p.
Volume Four: Transnational Corporations and Business Strategy.. 416 p.

Set B (Boxed set of 4 volumes. ISBN 0-415-08555-1. ,350):
Volume Five: International Financial Management. 400 p.
Volume Six: Organization of Transnational Corporations. 400 p.
Volume Seven: Governments and Transnational Corporations. 352 p.

Volume Eight: Transnational Corporations and International Trade and Payments. 320 p.

Set C (Boxed set of 4 volumes. ISBN 0-415-08556-X. ,350):
Volume Nine: Transnational Corporations and Regional Economic Integration.
331 p.
Volume Ten: Transnational Corporations and the Exploitation of Natural Resources. 397 p.
Volume Eleven: Transnational Corporations and Industrialization.
425 p.
Volume Twelve: Transnational Corporations in Services. 437 p.

Set D (Boxed set of 4 volumes. ISBN 0-415-08557-8. ,350):

Volume Thirteen: Cooperative Forms of Transnational Corporation Activity. 419 p.
Volume Fourteen: Transnational Corporations: Transfer Pricing and Taxation.
330 p.
Volume Fifteen: Transnational Corporations: Market Structure and Industrial Performance. 383 p.
Volume Sixteen: Transnational Corporations and Human Resources. 429 p.

Set E (Boxed set of 4 volumes. ISBN 0-415-08558-6. ,350):
Volume Seventeen: Transnational Corporations and Innovatory Activities. 447 p.
Volume Eighteen: Transnational Corporations and Technology Transfer to Developing Countries. 486 p.
Volume Nineteen: Transnational Corporations and National Law.
322 p.
Volume Twenty: Transnational Corporations: The International Legal Framework. 545 p.

D. Journals

Transnational Corporations (formerly The CTC Reporter).
Published three times a year. Annual subscription price: $45; individual issues $20.

ProInvest, a quarterly newsletter, available free of charge.

United Nations publications may be obtained from bookstores and distributors throughout the world. Please consult your bookstore or write to:

United Nations Publications

Sales Section   OR   Sales Section
Room DC2-0853   United Nations Office at Geneva
United Nations Secretariat   Palais des Nations
New York, NY 10017   CH-1211 Geneva 10
U.S.A.   Switzerland
Tel: (1-212) 963-8302 or   Tel: (41-22) 917-1234
(800) 253-9646   Fax: (41-22) 917-0123
Fax: (1-212) 963-3489   E-mail: unpubli@unog.ch
E-mail: publications@un.org

All prices are quoted in United States dollars.

For further information on the work of the Division on Investment, Technology and Enterprise Development, UNCTAD, please address inquiries to:

United Nations Conference on Trade and Development
Division on Investment, Technology and Enterprise Development
Palais des Nations, Room E-10069
CH-1211 Geneva 10
Switzerland
Telephone: (41-22) 907-5651
Telefax: (41-22) 907-0194
E-mail: natalia.guerra@unctad.org

QUESTIONNAIRE

Transfer of Technology

Sales No. E.01.II.D.33

In order to improve the quality and relevance of the work of the UNCTAD Division on Investment, Technology and Enterprise Development, it would be useful to receive the views of readers on this and other similar publications. It would therefore be greatly appreciated if you could complete the following questionnaire and return it to:

Readership Survey
UNCTAD Division on Investment, Technology and Enterprise
Development
United Nations Office at Geneva
Palais des Nations
Room E-10069
CH-1211 Geneva 10
Switzerland
Fax: 41-22 907-0194

1. Name and address of respondent (optional):

    _____

    _____

    _____

    _____

    _____

2. Which of the following best describes your area of work?

    Government ☐   Public enterprise ☐

    Private enterprise
    institution ☐   Academic or
                          research ☐

    International
    organization ☐   Media ☐

    Not-for-profit
    organization ☐   Other (specify)

3. In which country do you work? _____

4. What is your assessment of the contents of this publication?

    Excellent ☐   Adequate ☐

    Good ☐   Poor ☐

5. How useful is this publication to your work?

    Very useful ☐   Of some use ☐   Irrelevant ☐

6. Please indicate the three things you liked best about this publication:

7. Please indicate the three things you liked least about this publication:

8. If you have read more than the present publication of the UNCTAD Division on Investment, Technology and Enterprise Development, what is your overall assessment of them?

Consistently good ☐ Usually good, but with some exceptions ☐

Generally mediocre ☐ Poor ☐

9. On the average, how useful are these publications to you in your work?

Very useful ☐ Of some use ☐ Irrelevant ☐

10. Are you a regular recipient of **Transnational Corporations** (formerly **The CTC Reporter**), the Division's tri-annual refereed journal?

Yes ☐ No ☐

If not, please check here if you would like to receive a sample copy sent to the name and address you have given above ☐

302995417/

Printed at United Nations, Geneva
GE.01-53205–November 2001–3,715

United Nations publication
Sales No. E.01.II.D.33

UNCTAD/ITE/IIT/28

ISBN 92-1-112545-6